Horse Lover's Guide to
KENTUCKY

Horse Lover's Guide to
KENTUCKY

Patti Nickell

EP
ECLIPSE PRESS

LEXINGTON, KENTUCKY

Library of Congress Control Number: 2009922185

ISBN 978-1-58150-216-9

Printed in the United States
First Edition: 2009
Book design: Brian Turner
Cover photo: James Archambeault

a division of
Blood-Horse Publications
PUBLISHERS SINCE 1916

Who are the great sires and what are their great stories? Where are the best places to see them today — both on and off the track? In addition, you will get an insight into the non-horse related places and activities that Kentucky has to offer. For the purposes of this book, most of those places are located in the Bluegrass region of the state — between Lexington and Louisville — the epicenter of the Thoroughbred industry. There is, however, one chapter where I venture outside of Central Kentucky, crossing the state to visit Kentucky's top 10 attractions (very subjective, I admit).

For anyone interested in the commonwealth and its legendary equine symbol, *A Horse Lover's Guide to Kentucky* is a fitting companion.

— *Patti Nickell*

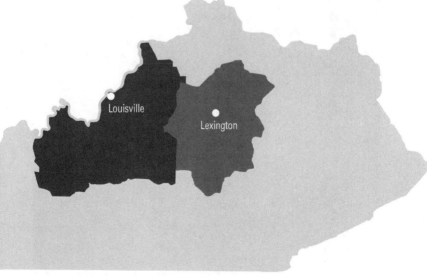

Kentucky Department of Travel

Contents

Preface

Americans have always loved their animals — both domestic and feral. If you have any doubts, just look at the number of states that tie their identity — at least in part — to a member of the animal kingdom. Our fifty states have paid tribute to a wide range of animals — from the buffalo to the beaver and the retriever to the raccoon. California was briefly known as the Bear Republic and Texas is recognized far and wide for its Longhorns.

However, if you want to talk about more majestic animals, nothing can compare with the horse, which has been symbolic of the Commonwealth of Kentucky for two and a half centuries. Whether it is the state's only native breed, the Saddlebred, or the fast-action trotters and pacers known as Standardbreds, or the Thoroughbreds breaking from the starting gate, these magnificent creatures have come to define the Bluegrass State, especially Lexington, which has become known as "the Horse Capital of the World."

In this book you'll discover everything you want to know about the Kentucky–horse connection: Where are they bred and where do they breed? Where do they race and where do they retire?

1

A Brief Overview of Kentucky's Founding

In 1750 the area now known as Kentucky was still part of the Commonwealth of Virginia, although remote from the civilized English society of the Tidewater. Early settlers believed its Indian name, Kain-tuck-ee, translated to "dark and bloody ground;" a less dramatic but more accurate translation comes from the Wyandot nation — "land of tomorrow." While not exactly the lurid location described in pulp fiction novels known as "penny-dreadfuls," the area was, nevertheless, a remote wilderness used as a hunting preserve by the Shawnee in the north and the Cherokee in the south.

An entire generation of TV viewers came to believe that it was Daniel Boone, as conceived by Walt Disney and portrayed by Fess Parker — complete with coonskin cap and a fictitious Indian companion by the name of Mingo — who was the first to arrive in Kentucky. Disney's version made good TV, but history books tell us it was the lesser known Dr. Thomas Walker, not Boone, who was the first white man to set foot on Kentucky soil.

Although relatively little of Walker's life is documented, it is known that he developed his wanderlust while serving as personal physician to Virginia landowner Peter Jefferson, father of President Thomas Jefferson, and himself a noted explorer. It is presumed that under the elder Jefferson's tutelage, Walker's skill as an explorer and surveyor blossomed. His first attempt to reach Kentucky in 1743 failed, with his party getting only as far as present-day Kingsport, Tennessee.

He was more successful on his second attempt, which began in March of 1750, and followed a convoluted route from Virginia, down into North Carolina, across into Tennessee, and back up to Virginia before finally reaching the Cumberland Gap on April 13, 1750. He recorded his find in a diary entry:

"We went four miles to a large creek, which we called Cedar, being a branch of Bear Grass, and from thence six miles to Cave Gap (Cumberland Gap.) On the north side of the gap is a large spring which falls very fast, and just above the spring is a small entrance to a large cave which the spring runs through. The gap may be seen at a considerable distance, and there is no other, that I know of, except one about two miles to the north of it, which does not appear to be so low as the other."

Perhaps it was Walker's wishy-washy stance on whether there was actually one gap or two that kept him from earning the place in history he deserved (although he is credited with drawing Walker's Line, the first boundary between Kentucky and Tennessee). He faded into relative obscurity, while Boone, coming later to the party ... 19 years later to be exact ... became a Kentucky legend.

THE BOONE YEARS

Daniel Boone, though he cannot be credited with founding Kentucky, was nonetheless instrumental in the settlement of the commonwealth. In 1769, he and five companions (none of them the stalwart Mingo of the TV series) first found their way through the Cumberland Gap into Kentucky. He must have liked what he saw as it was three years before this Odysseus of the frontier made it back to his loyal wife Rebecca, safely tucked away in North Carolina's fertile Yadkin River Valley. Dan'l's siren song, unlike that of his Homeric counterpart, was not of the human variety, but that of the land. When he did return to Rebecca, it was only to tell her to pack up the kids and the possessions as they were trading in the farm for the frontier.

Back to Kentucky they went, and for the next few years Boone made several failed attempts to establish a base. Finally, in the spring of 1775, the intrepid explorer and his party reached the lofty palisades of the Kentucky River, in the central part of the state near present-day Richmond, and agreed that it was as good a spot as any for their permanent settlement. (One could argue that it was the long-suffering Rebecca who finally put her foot down and refused to budge another inch.)

At any rate, the river was a good source of water and the fertile grassland was ideal for farming and raising livestock. Knowing the area was used by the Shawnee as a hunting ground, Boone and party decided the first order of business was to construct a fort as a temporary residence for settlers while they built their own homes, and as a permanent protection against the Shawnee.

The layout of the original fort was a rectangle of crude cabins running parallel to the river, eventually consisting of these one-story cabins, with two-story blockhouses anchoring each of the fort's four corners, with a wall between the cabins to serve as a defense against attack. It proved a durable design as Fort Boonesborough withstood several major Indian attacks, including a 10-day siege in 1778 during which the settlers held off a combined force of more than 400 Indians and 12 of their French allies. Though occupied for less than 50 years, Fort Boonesborough looms large in the state's history, serving as protection for settlers pouring through the Cumberland Gap along the Wilderness Road.

Daniel Boone's pioneering efforts established his legacy in the state, and today tombstones bearing his name and that of Rebecca mark graves overlooking the Kentucky River in the state capitol of Frankfort. Note: There is some disagreement as to whether the bodies in the Frankfort cemetery are really those of the Boones; some skeptics have claimed that the real remains were never returned to Kentucky but are in Missouri where the couple lived out their days after leaving Kentucky to push farther west. Though not his official epitaph, Boone had been quoted as saying, "I was happy in the midst of dangers and inconveniences." Rebecca remained silent on the subject.

Note: Boonesborough was not the first permanent fort established in Kentucky. Fort Harrod in Harrodsburg had been built a year earlier in 1774 by pioneer and marksman James Harrod. Though not as well-remembered by history as Boone, Harrod was just as fascinating — his life equal parts adventure, tragedy, and mystery. He lost his first wife, brother, and stepson in Indian raids, and disappeared himself on a hunting trip in 1792, never to be heard from again.

While Fort Boonesborough benefits from the cachet surrounding Daniel Boone, Fort Harrod is equally important, being the site of both a memorial to George Rogers Clark, the founder of Louisville, and the Lincoln Marriage Temple, where Thomas Lincoln and Nancy Hanks, the parents of Abraham Lincoln, were married.

DID YOU KNOW

While much of the rest of the state was still frontier, Lexington, because of its sophistication and culture, was known as "the Athens of the West."

THE FOUNDING OF LEXINGTON

The Bluegrass of Central Kentucky is known throughout the world for the pristine beauty of its landscape, and the region's major city, Lexington, is the jewel in the crown. However, the area was wilderness in 1775 when William McConnell and his fellow frontiersmen — explorers from Pennsylvania's upper Monongahela River region — camped alongside a natural spring while surveying the newly opened American frontier for possible settlement.

One can only imagine the scene on that June night. The men were sitting around the hearth of their crude shelter, perhaps enjoying a smoke and a tipple of whiskey, when a rider from nearby Fort Boonesborough interrupted their reverie. He was bringing word of a battle that had been waged two months earlier in a small Massachusetts town where the Colonial militia had bested the cream of the British regulars.

In a burst of patriotic spirit, the men chose Lexington as the name of their settlement in homage to that Revolutionary War battle of Lexington and Concord. McConnell garnered some recognition as well, as the beautiful natural springs where he and his men were camped became known as McConnell Springs — the official birthplace of Lexington and today listed on the National Register of Historic Places.

From that humble (and spontaneous) beginning, Lexington quickly rose to such prominence that while the rest of the state was still a bloody frontier, it was known as "the Athens of the West," home to the first university west of the Allegheny Mountains (Transylvania), the first performance of a Beethoven symphony in the United States (Symphony No. 7), and a bevy of distinguished citizens — statesman Henry Clay, Confederate general John Hunt Morgan, portrait painter Matthew Jouett, and Mary Todd Lincoln, wife of the 16th president. Most importantly, it was to become the epicenter of a flourishing and world-renowned Thoroughbred industry.

... AND LOUISVILLE

Three years after Lexington was founded at McConnell Springs, George Rogers Clark, a colonel in the Continental army, was conducting a campaign against the British north of the Ohio River in what is present-day Illinois. Arriving at the Falls of the Ohio in 1778, he set up a communications post that was dubbed Corn Island.

The following year, settlers started arriving in droves, thus establishing a permanent settlement. Feeling that Corn Island lacked the proper cachet for what they hoped would be a thriving metropolis, the settlers named their new town Louisville in honor of the French King Louis XVI, who was providing francs and French soldiers to aid the colonists in their conflict with the British.

In 1780 Thomas Jefferson, then-governor of Virginia, approved Louisville's charter and the small post originally founded by Clark was on its way to becoming a major hub on the Ohio. Interesting historical note: Twenty-five years after its original founding, Clark's younger brother, William, and his partner Meriwether Lewis, set out on their Manifest Destiny (and Louisiana Purchase) journey to the Pacific from those same Falls of the Ohio.

Although generally considered to be in the middle tier of American cities — size and population-wise — Louisville has produced an eclectic group of native sons and daughters: Louis Brandeis, the first Jewish Supreme Court Justice; boxing legend Muhammad Ali; film stars Irene Dunne and Victor Mature, newswoman Diane Sawyer, and writers Hunter S. Thompson and Sue Grafton. With a more dubious claim to fame, other Louisvillians include Foster Brooks, the comedian who gained fame as "the Lovable Lush," and photographer Larry Birkhead, better known as the winner of the Anna Nicole Smith baby-daddy sweepstakes.

In addition, the city was the site of such notable events as the first public viewing of Edison's light bulb, the penning of the song Happy Birthday by two Louisville sisters, the first human hand transplant, and the first self-contained artificial heart transplant.

Overshadowing them all, however, is what is billed as "the most exciting two minutes in sports," — the Run for the Roses, held every year on the first Saturday in May. To bring it full circle, it was Meriwether Lewis Clark, Jr., the grandson of William, who nearly a century after Louisville's founding was responsible for organizing the first Kentucky Derby in May 1875.

2

The History of the Horse in Kentucky

"You were a Lord if you had a horse."

— D.H. LAWRENCE

Up until the expeditions of Thomas Walker and Daniel Boone, there were no permanent residents of the Bluegrass region — human or equine. The land itself was lush — described by photographer James Archambeault in the preface to his book *Kentucky Horse Country* as "covered with rich, brown, fertile soil that a simple hand spade cut through like warm butter." So rich was the land, in fact, — not just in soil, but in forests and grasslands — that the Native Americans of the region agreed all tribes would use it as a hunting ground, but none would live there.

With the coming of the settlers, all that changed. Not only was the land valuable, but so was the ancient limestone cap that lay beneath. The same calcium in the limestone that fertilized the topsoil was instrumental in developing strong bones in horses. Thus, the area became a paradise for breeding horses. The Thoroughbred, which thrives on the rich Kentucky pasture land and has become the state's equine symbol, was not, however, the first breed to call Kentucky home.

KENTUCKY'S ONLY NATIVE BREED

That honor belongs to the American Saddlebred, which came to the commonwealth by a rather circuitous route. A breed of horse known as the Narragansett Pacer, developed in New England, was crossed with the English Thoroughbred; their progeny became the ancestors of what we know today as the saddle horse, used for both work and recreation.

These horses accompanied the pioneers who followed Walker and Boone through the Cumberland Gap, and as Kentucky plantations developed, so did the Saddlebred. So famous did Kentucky become for producing fine saddle horses that in the War of 1812, Kentuckians, combining their own fighting skills with the stamina of their hardy mounts, became the scourge of the British and their Indian allies.

Kentuckians were also at the front in the Mexican-American War, and by the time of its outbreak in 1846, their American saddle horse mounts had become an established breed. During the Civil War nearly every officer on both sides of the conflict rode a Saddlebred, including Ulysses S. Grant on Cincinnati and Robert E. Lee on Traveler. Indeed, the horses of the period had become so identified with the state that they were known as "Kentucky Saddlers."

But the saddle horse was bred for pursuits other than war. The breed was a great favorite in the show ring — the first record of such an event was in Lexington in 1817.

DID YOU KNOW

The American Saddlebred is the only breed native to Kentucky; it originated in the 19th century as a direct descendant of Denmark, a Thoroughbred in Confederate General John Hunt Morgan's cavalry.

The American Saddlebred, with its combination of beauty, strength, and speed, has been well-suited to its various roles down through the centuries, from carrying Paul Revere on his famous ride to herding cattle in the American West to functioning as the horse of choice for recreational riders.

THE THOROUGHBRED: PRIDE OF THE BLUEGRASS

The regal Thoroughbred, symbol of Kentucky's Bluegrass region, can trace its ancestry back to three stallions — the Byerley Turk, the Godolphin Arabian, and the Darley Arabian — all of which were imported to England in the 17th and 18th centuries. Today, every Thoroughbred registered with The Jockey Club can trace its lineage back to one of these famous sires.

As noted earlier, the migration of settlers to Kentucky, bringing their horses with them, led to the sowing of the first seeds that would blossom into a mighty industry. The breed may have originated in England and been brought first to the New England colonies, but it reached maturity in the sweet bluegrass of the commonwealth.

Lexington, the undisputed epicenter of America's Thoroughbred industry, could only briefly have been considered a "one-horse town" — back in 1779 when the first Thoroughbred to be used strictly for racing purposes was brought to the city. A decade later horses would outnumber the people who gathered to watch them run on the state's first racetrack, which ran right through the heart of downtown Lexington.

That track bore little resemblance to today's state-of-the-art version. Known as the Commons, the one-block stretch near present day Race Street drew enthusiastic horsemen to wager on their favorite mounts. Their enthusiasm, however, was not shared by the local citizenry, who deemed the sometimes out-of-control horses and riders a "safety hazard."

The complaints led to a more organized, formal meet at the Commons (there is record of a three-day race meet being held there as far back as 1791), and, to oversee it, the formation of the commonwealth's first Jockey Club. Formed at a local tavern in 1797 (Kentucky statesman Henry Clay was among the founding members), it received official status as the Kentucky Jockey Club in 1809.

FYI: If Lexington is generally credited with having the state's first racetrack — crude though it was — the William Whitley House in Stanford in the southeastern part of the state was the first to have the more formal, oval-shaped track we are familiar with today. It is believed that this track introduced the American practice of racing counter-clockwise — the exact opposite of the British, who raced in a clockwise direction.

If Kentucky's first racecourse was built in Lexington, its first official horse farm was started not in the Bluegrass but near Louisville. In 1786, William Christian, a brother-in-law of Virginia Governor Patrick Henry (of "give me liberty or give me death" fame) had barely hung out the shingle on his farm on Beargrass Creek, just outside of present-day Louisville, when he was slain by marauding Indians — on, of all things, a horse raid. But if Louisville edged out Lexington in creating the first horse farm, it didn't take Lexington long to catch up. By the mid-19th century, Central Kentucky had become a mecca for breeding horses. Still, it would take the greatest conflict in American history to cement the city's future as the Horse Capital of the World.

THE RISE OF KENTUCKY'S THOROUGHBRED INDUSTRY

Today Lexington is to the Thoroughbred industry what Hollywood is to the entertainment industry, Detroit to the automobile industry, and Las Vegas to the gaming industry. That's why it may come as something of a surprise to learn that prior to the Civil

War, Tennessee was better known for its Thoroughbreds than for its famed walking horses, and that it was Nashville, not Lexington, which was primed to become the Thoroughbred capital of the world.

North central Tennessee — in common with Central Kentucky — has vast natural deposits of limestone just below the ground's surface, which enrich the grass as well as the rivers and waterways that run through the area. Horses benefited from the calcium-rich limestone, giving them an edge over those bred in other parts of the country. During the Antebellum period the leading farm of the day was Belle Meade, owned by General William Giles Harding.

In the mid-19th century, Harding amassed land holdings of 5,400 acres, part of which was used to breed and train champion Thoroughbred horses. So successful was he that in 1839 Harding penned a letter to the editor of the *American Turf Registry*, extolling the virtues of Belle Meade as a breeding establishment. He wrote, "Blood stock here is all the go. To be without it is to be out of fashion and destitute of taste."

Breeding on the farm was still going strong in the 1880s when the new owner, Harding's son-in-law, former Confederate General William Hicks Jackson, purchased a stallion, Iroquois, who was the first American-bred winner of the English Derby. However, the early 20th century brought both the death of Jackson and the dissolution of the farm, which was sold shortly thereafter.

What was once the finest Thoroughbred farm in Tennessee (Kentucky Derby winners such as Secretariat, Funny Cide, and Barbaro can trace their bloodlines back to Belle Meade breeding stock) is now an upscale Nashville suburb.

It is no exaggeration to say that Harding's counterpart in Kentucky, Robert A. Alexander, owner of Woodburn Stud in Woodford County, is considered the father of Kentucky's Thoroughbred industry. Inheriting the property, a former land grant, from his Scottish immigrant father, Alexander succeeded in bringing it to the pinnacle of breeding and racing success in the years just prior to the Civil War. He was the first to establish a system for breeding horses, and one of his stallions, Lexington, was America's leading sire for nearly two decades. Another stallion, Preakness, gave the second leg of the Triple Crown its name. Although best known for its incomparable roster of Thoroughbreds (four Kentucky Derby winners, four Preakness winners, and 10 Belmont Stakes winners), Woodburn is also credited with being the birthplace of the Standardbred (see separate entry).

Today, part of the original Woodburn makes up Airdrie Stud, owned by former Kentucky Governor Brereton Jones and his wife Libby, a descendant of the Alexanders.

WAR DISRUPTS THE INDUSTRY

With the outbreak of the Civil War, Tennessee joined the Confederacy while Kentucky, despite having strong pro-Confederate sympathies, especially in the Bluegrass, managed to remain neutral, and this, ultimately, was what led to the transference of the Thoroughbred industry from Nashville north to Lexington.

While both Belle Meade and Woodburn, thanks to the efforts of Harding and Alexander, became sanctuaries of sorts, saving many valuable racehorses from army service, many more were captured and pressed into service. In one of the most famous of these raids (October 22, 1864), the notorious guerilla leader Sue Mundy stole six Thoroughbreds from Woodburn's training stable, including Asteroid and Norwich, both offspring of the great sire Lexington.

Although recovered, the horses were again threatened just four months later when Mundy — this time under orders from Captain William Quantrill, another Confederate guerilla — raided Wood-

DID YOU KNOW

There has only been one horse to win the Triple Crown while undefeated — Seattle Slew.

burn a second time. Once more, he got away with Norwich (who once again was recovered), but Asteroid was saved by the quick thinking of his trainer, who substituted an inferior horse for the great stallion. That trainer, an African-American named Ansel Williamson, would — a decade later — go on to train the first Kentucky Derby winner, Aristides.

If the farms in the Lexington area had to worry about the threat of guerilla raids, the farms around Nashville suffered a fate even more dire. Now occupied by Union troops, Nashville-area horse farms, Belle Meade included, became the spoils of war. The Tennessee Thoroughbred industry, in common with the vanquished South's other industries, suffered a severe setback, leaving the door open for its neighbor to the north.

That is not to say Lexington's prominence happened overnight. Not only had area breeders lost valuable horses in the conflict but many had themselves been killed in the service of the Confederacy. The war had also destroyed some racetracks and sharply curtailed activities at those that had survived. Lexington's own racetrack had been in use as an army camp during the war years.

Still, two factors stood out in determining the return to prominence of Central Kentucky's horse industry. As already mentioned, one was the herculean effort of Woodburn to salvage as many horses as possible from being conscripted by the Union and Confederate armies. The second was the equally herculean effort of Lexington — not the city, but its namesake stallion.

As a racehorse, Lexington won six of seven starts and retired as the third-leading money winner at that time. During his stud career, a majority of which was spent at Woodburn, Lexington sired 600 foals, a third of which became winners on the track (among them Aristides, the first winner of the Kentucky Derby). Another of his progeny was the aforementioned Cincinnati, Ulysses Grant's favorite horse, whom the general was astride when he accepted Lee's surrender at Appomattox Courthouse.

In the post-Civil War years, most Thoroughbred racing was held at northern tracks such as Saratoga Springs in upstate New York and Monmouth Park in New Jersey with horses that had been stolen from southern farms. For all intents and purposes, the South's Thoroughbred industry had been destroyed, the exception being Central Kentucky. By the war's end, Woodburn's Alexander had been credited both with creating the post-war American Thoroughbred market and raising the standards of the trotting horse market.

Today, Central Kentucky is indeed the Thoroughbred capital of the world, and Woodburn was the prototype for some 450 Thoroughbred farms in the Lexington area alone, including such legendary names as Calumet, Darby Dan, Claiborne, Three Chimneys, and Gainesway.

THE BIRTH OF A TRADITION

Today, Louisville's Churchill Downs is one of the most famous racetracks in the world, and the Kentucky Derby is arguably the world's most famous race. Not bad, considering that Churchill Downs was started by a gentleman — if indeed that is the right word — whose obsession with racing, as well as other vices, caused his wife to leave him, whose boorish behavior eventually got him demoted to the position of steward at the very track he helped found, and whose compulsive gambling led to his suicide. Even more surprising was the fact that the first Kentucky Derby couldn't manage any better than the third drawing card at the inaugural race meet.

Meriwether Lewis Clark Jr., or Lutie as he was known to Louisville society in the 1870s, returned from a grand tour of Europe with the idea of building a racetrack and using the pari-mutuel wagering system he had observed at French tracks to eliminate the bookmaking practices common in America. He never completely succeeded at the latter, but the former was helped along considerably by the fact that his father had married into the Churchill family who owned 300 acres of prime Louisville land.

A portion of this land was set aside in 1873 for the Louisville Jockey Club and Driving Park Association, whose prominent members came up with the necessary scratch — $32,000 — to build a racetrack that opened, with great fanfare, two years later on May 17, 1875. In a twist of irony straight out of an O. Henry short story, the Derby race wasn't planned as the drawing card, with two other races, the Louisville Cup and the Gentleman's Cup, considered more important. But in the Derby race, when a three-year-old colt named Aristides set a new mile-and-a-half record, the crowd erupted in frenzy, and a tradition was born.

Aristides took his place in sporting history, but Lutie fared less well. Despite his track venture being declared a success from the beginning, Lewis' unpleasant personality and arrogance alienated him from both his family and the rest of Louisville's genteel "horse set." Indeed, the track became known as "Churchill's downs" in a snide reference to Lutie's downfall.

Still, there's no denying his contribution to the Thoroughbred industry, as he presided over the first American Turf Congress, out of which came many of the racing rules still observed today, and he had the idea for the Great American Stallion Stake — a precursor to the present-day Breeders' Cup.

But in a scenario worthy of author Damon Runyon, whose characters were often gamblers who went from riches to rags, Lewis spent his last years as a vagabond, roving from city to city, toiling as a steward at regional tracks. With his days in the limelight over and gambling debts piling up, he committed suicide in 1899. The Louisville Jockey Club went through a painful metamorphosis of its own, surviving virtual bankruptcy in the late 1890s and a decade more of uncertainty before the gleaming twin spires of Churchill Downs became a symbol of Thoroughbred racing's highest echelon.

... AND THEN CAME KEENELAND

It was only fitting that Lexington, dubbed "the horse capital of the world," would have its own Thoroughbred racetrack to equal Churchill Downs. That first track, known as the Commons, was the precursor to another track in downtown Lexington a half-century later. Between 1828 and 1834, the Kentucky Association, which had been formed to promote breeding and racing in the Bluegrass, accumulated 65 acres of land at what is now 5th and Race streets. On this land, they built a one-mile dirt track, complete with grandstand and stables.

What followed was six decades of success before financial problems led to the sale of the track in 1890. The new owners, faced with the economic Panic of 1893, fared no better than the previ-

DID YOU KNOW

All Thoroughbred horses celebrate
their birthday on the same day.
January 1 is the universal birth date of all
Thoroughbreds in the northern hemisphere.
(In the southern hemisphere it is August 1.)

ous ones. At one race in 1896, they were able to draw only two entries, a situation that did not go unnoticed by the *New York Times*, which called it a farce. The track continued its up-and-down existence — under a succession of owners — until 1933 when it finally closed.

America was in the throes of the Great Depression, but in Lexington there was cause for celebration. The Kentucky Association track was gone, having been dismantled in 1935, but out of the ashes of that track rose the phoenix of an even greater one. That same year horseman Jack Keene sold 147 acres of farmland six miles west of downtown Lexington to the newly formed Keeneland Association. Keeneland Race Course officially opened in 1936.

From the outset, the non-profit track has embraced the betterment of Thoroughbred racing and breeding as its mission. Keeneland's motto — "racing as it was meant to be" — continues to express the philosophy of the track's first president, Hal Price Headley. "We want a place where those who love horses can come and picnic with us and thrill to the sport of the Bluegrass. We are not running a race plant to hear the click of the mutuel machines," he said.

Indeed, Keeneland conducts racing in a park-like setting, and its grounds and buildings are so beautiful the track is listed on the National Register of Historic places. Traditions are important here, and even today people dress up to go to the races. Not until 1997 did Keeneland install a public address system for broadcasting the races, using only the tote board to announce winners. The highly knowledgeable Keeneland race crowd liked it that way — believing that if you knew your racing silks, there was no need for a PA system.

Change may come slowly to Keeneland, but in one important area it took the lead. In 2006, the original dirt track was replaced with Polytrack, an artificial all-weather surface deemed to be safer for both horses and riders.

Today, Keeneland, with its picturesque setting — stone club-house, magnolia and dogwood trees bursting with creamy blossoms, and manicured paddock area — holds two annual race meets — in April and in October. One of the most important Kentucky Derby prep races, the Toyota Blue Grass Stakes, is a major feature of the spring meet, and a series of races in the fall meet leads up to the Breeders' Cup Championship every November.

The yearling sale held every September in the Keeneland sales pavilion is one of the most important Thoroughbred sales in the world. Over the years, countless winners of the Kentucky Derby, Breeders' Cup, Epsom Derby, Irish Derby, and French Derby have been purchased at the Keeneland sales.

STANDARDBRED RACING AND THE RED MILE

If Thoroughbreds came first in the hearts of Kentuckians, they were closely followed by the Standardbreds, or trotting horses. Unlike Thoroughbreds, which were developed in England by crossing draft horses with Arabians, Standardbreds are altogether American, although both breeds share common ancestry. Hambletonian, perhaps the most famous Standardbred in history, was sired by an English Thoroughbred that had been imported to America.

Originally used for practical rather than sporting purposes, the Standardbred as a trotter was first introduced to Kentucky in 1854 by James B. Clay, a son of Henry Clay (an earlier experiment with a stallion named Abdullah had been unsuccessful). These horses, usually heavier than Thoroughbreds and with a more serene temperament, are known for their skill in racing in harness and pulling a sulky at a trot or pace, rather than under a saddle at a gallop. The breed's name came from the fact that these horses had to be able to trot a mile inside the "standard" time of two minutes, thirty seconds.

Almost from the beginning, Standardbreds were looked down on as "second-class horses" by Thoroughbred breeders, in much the same manner as cattlemen looked down on sheepherders on the western ranges. While Thoroughbred racing, dubbed the "Sport of Kings," had an aura of wealth and privilege surrounding it, harness racing had sprung from the working classes of small towns and gained popularity in county fairs across the country. With a few exceptions — Lexington's Red Mile became a showcase for the nation's top trotters — Standardbreds continued to be thought of as "Kentucky's other horse."

The first Kentucky Derby had been run just five months earlier when on September 28, 1875, the Great Fall Trots at The Red Mile opened in Lexington with surprisingly little fanfare considering the devotion shown by horse-mad Kentuckians for breeds of all types. The initial lack of response was explained when it was later discovered that the race organizers had neglected to publicize the track's grand opening. Needless to say, subsequent meets were far better attended.

Today, The Red Mile — so named because of its one-mile length and the rich red clay of the track — has both tradition and a flourishing schedule working in its favor. As for tradition, it is the second-oldest harness track in the world and the site of more world-record harness racing performances than any other track. As far as the schedule is concerned, the annual Standardbred season culminates in the Kentucky Futurity, the third leg of trotting's Triple Crown, and after a decade-long absence, 2004 signaled the return of Quarter Horse racing to the track. In addition, The Red Mile offers year-round simulcasts from tracks around the country, as well as various other horse-related events.

The state's other harness tracks have not fared so well. Louisville

Downs was purchased by Churchill Downs which converted it into a training track for Thoroughbreds, leaving Riverside Downs in Western Kentucky as the state's only other trotting track.

The waning of Standardbred racing coincided with the flight of the Standardbred breeding industry from the state during the 1970s and '80s. Yet for nearly a century — from the late 1800s to the 1970s, Standardbred breeding was conducted on a large scale in Central Kentucky. Many of today's Thoroughbred farms got their start as Standardbred farms, including Airdrie Stud, Hamburg Place, and even Calumet, which has the distinction of having bred both Kentucky Derby and Hambletonian champions. Almahurst, founded on an 18th-century land grant, produced both Thoroughbreds — 1918 Kentucky Derby winner Exterminator — and Standardbreds — the 1930s trotter Greyhound — before changing hands and becoming a Thoroughbred operation, now known as Ramsey Farm.

One farm — Castleton — has switched breeds no fewer than five times. It started as the Thoroughbred operation of Senator John Breckenridge in the 18th century, and in the mid-1800s his son-in-law converted it to a Standardbred farm. It switched again in the late 1800s and became the greatest Thoroughbred farm of the time, producing such stallions as Domino, Spendthrift, Black Toney, and Ben Brush. For more than half a century, from the 1920s until 2001, the farm was one of the Bluegrass's most famous Standardbred operations, under two different owners. In 2001, an Irish entrepreneur, Tony Ryan, purchased the property, renamed it Castleton Lyons and brought it full circle — as once again it is a Thoroughbred farm.

One of the earliest of Lexington's famous farms, Walnut Hall, has always devoted itself to Standardbreds and is today the nation's oldest successful trotting farm, having been in the same family since

1892. In 1972 current owner Margaret Jewett sold a portion of the original farm begun by her great-grandfather L.V. Harkness to the state for the creation of the Kentucky Horse Park.

Despite some notable exceptions, as the Thoroughbred industry waxed, the Standardbred industry waned, with the nadir being the 1970s and '80s when a host of incentive programs succeeded in luring the best Standardbreds from Kentucky to such states as New Jersey, New York, Illinois, and Ohio.

While these states brought out the proverbial carrot — in the form of higher purses and other enticements — Kentucky tumbled to the bottom, with one of the lowest purse structures of any other harness-racing state.

OTHER BREEDS

Where did the Rocky Mountain Horse originate? It sounds like a question from *Jeopardy*'s Stupid Answer category. If you said … um … the Rocky Mountains, you will get that "tsk-tsk" from Alex Trebek, but if you said Kentucky, then give yourself $100.

On Sam Tuttle's farm in the Eastern Kentucky community of Spout Springs, a placid, sure-footed horse by the name of Tobe became the founding sire of the current breed. Tobe continued to sire offspring until the ripe old age of 37, and some of the descendants of those horses make up the present Rocky Mountain breed.

Known for their gentle and docile nature, as well as their sure-footedness, the Rocky Mountain Horse is said to be the perfect mount for beginning and/or tentative riders. Tobe — then known as Old Tobe — proved the truth of that in the 1960s when he carried riders up and down the trails of Natural Bridge State Park where Sam held a concession for horseback rides.

Similarly, when one thinks of Quarter Horses, he usually thinks of Texas or Colorado rather than Kentucky, but in recent years the Kentucky Breeders Incentive Fund has succeeded in bringing an influx of Quarter Horse stallions to the state. The fund is a state economic development program passed by the Kentucky General Assembly in 2005 to stimulate the growth of the Quarter Horse breeding industry through special incentives to owners and breeders.

The Quarter Horse is known as both a racehorse (it excels at sprinting short distances and can easily outpace other breeds at distances of up to a quarter of a mile) and as a performer in rodeos and horse shows.

3

Bluegrass Thoroughbred Horse Farms

"A horse! A horse! My kingdom for a horse!"

— WILLIAM SHAKESPEARE, RICHARD III

Few places in the world can be defined by a single commodity: the Champagne region of France, California's Napa Valley wine country, and St. Andrews, Scotland, the "home of golf," come to mind. To that select list add Kentucky's Bluegrass region. Home to the world's largest concentration of Thoroughbred horses, it immediately conjures up images of red-trimmed barns and emerald hills ringed by white fences behind which mares and their wobbly-legged foals cavort.

The cast of human characters involved in Thoroughbred racing and breeding is almost as fascinating as their equine treasures. Among past and present Thoroughbred farm owners have been business tycoons (Cornelius Vanderbilt Whitney, founder of Pan American Airlines, and John Galbreath, past owner of the Pittsburgh Pirates), cosmetics queens (Elizabeth Arden), ambassadors (William Farish), and royalty (sheikhs from Dubai and a Saudi prince). Bluegrass horse country exudes a rarefied air of wealth and privilege that affects all who breathe it.

The Lexington area alone is home to some 450 Thoroughbred farms, from "boutique" operations with a few stallions or mares to the giants of the industry, where Kentucky Derby champions and major stakes winners retire to stud.

Visitors to the Bluegrass can see these farms several different ways: a self-guided driving tour — maps indicating farm locations can be picked up at the Lexington Convention & Visitors Bureau (301 East Vine Street, 859-233-1221, www.visitlex.com) — or a guided farm tour (see list of companies providing horse farm tours on pages 48–50).

With the former you'll see beautiful landscapes, and if you come at the right time of year, mares and foals in the pastures. Except for rare exceptions, though, you will not be allowed on the farms. However, tour companies have permission to take visitors on a "behind-the-scenes" look at some of these magnificent farms, often with a chance to meet equine celebrities and even, for the non-squeamish, to see an actual breeding.

Following are some of the most famous Bluegrass farms, some steeped in history and tradition, and others bankrolled by present-day fortunes. Some are open to the public; others are not. If you are interested in a particular farm, check with the Convention & Visitors Bureau to see if the farm is on a tour or can be seen by appointment.

ASHFORD STUD

Coolmore, based in County Tipperary, Ireland, is one of the world's largest Thoroughbred breeding operation, with branches in Australia's Hunter Valley and Ashford Stud in Kentucky's Bluegrass region. Coolmore was founded by John Magnier, who still retains ownership, and his father-in-law, the late M.V. O'Brien, who has been ranked as the greatest trainer of the 20th century in Britain and Ireland.

Ashford Stud's 2,000 acres are lush — perhaps more reminiscent of landscaped parkland than a working horse farm — and its stone buildings, with the signature blue trim, are reminiscent of those at its sister location in Ireland. It is also one of the biggest farms in Kentucky, based on the number of stallions. Among those stallions are 2000 Kentucky Derby winner Fusaichi Pegasus, 1995 Derby winner Thunder Gulch, and Giant's Causeway, a son of Storm Cat and considered by many one of the best young sires in the world.

Note: Coolmore was a pioneer in shuttling stallions between the Northern and Southern hemispheres to take advantage of the alternating breeding seasons. Some of Ashford Stud's stallions travel to the Australia location following the Kentucky breeding season, so you have to plan your visit in season (February to June) if you expect to find them "at home."

5095 Frankfort Rd. (U.S 60), Versailles. (859) 873-7088.

www.coolmore.com

CALUMET FARM

Arguably the most famous Thoroughbred farm in the world, Calumet has produced a record eight Kentucky Derby winners, two Triple Crown winners (Whirlaway and Citation), the 1990 leading sire in America (Alydar), and 11 National Museum of Racing and Hall of Fame equine inductees.

Calumet sits on Versailles Road (US Highway 60) with Keeneland to its west and Blue Grass Airport across the highway. Surrounded by miles of gleaming white fences, the farm is dotted with picturesque white barns trimmed in red, the colors said to come from the packaging for Calumet Baking Powder, the business owned by the farm's founder, William Wright Sr.

What Wright established in 1924, initially as a Standardbred farm before his son Warren converted it to a Thoroughbred farm in the early 1930s, reached its pinnacle in the 1940s and '50s when Calumet's trophy cases overflowed with the hardware earned by its prize colts and fillies. That success continued through the 1970s.

One of the most endearing stories about a Calumet horse involved the great Alydar. In his autobiography, *My Life*, James E. (Ted) Bassett, the former president of Keeneland Race Course, writes about how in the 1978 Blue Grass Stakes at Keeneland, jockey Jorge Velasquez rode Alydar up to the rail where his owner Lucille Wright Markey was standing.

"Bow for your lady," Velasquez commanded and Alydar lowered his head before proceeding to win the Blue Grass Stakes by 13 lengths. Here in the Bluegrass, even the horses are taught good manners.

After Mrs. Markey's death and a period of scandal and decline in the late 1980s and early '90s, the farm was sold at public auction in 1992 to Polish-Canadian businessman Henryk de Kwiatkowski for a final bid of $17 million dollars. Taking his stewardship seriously, the new owner spent millions more restoring Calumet to the splendor of its glory years, promising to forever keep "the fences white and the fields lush." Calumet had been saved, and for that de Kwiatkowski achieved folk hero status in the Bluegrass.

Following de Kwiatkowski's death in 2003, ownership passed to his family, which along with a board of trustees, is working to bring Calumet back to its former racing prominence.

3301 Versailles Rd., (US Highway 60), Lexington. (859) 231-8272.
www.calumetfarm.com

CLAIBORNE FARM

Claiborne is probably best known as being the home and burial place of 1973 Triple Crown winner Secretariat, but the farm has as rich a history as any other in the Bluegrass. Among its storied champions — either born or retired to stud on the farm — were Bold Ruler, Gallant Fox, Buckpasser, Riva Ridge, Nijinsky, and Unbridled — a veritable "Who's Who" of Derby and major stakes winners.

Since Claiborne's founding in 1910, the Hancock family has presided over the 3,500 beautifully landscaped acres stretching from its massive stone gates to the town of Paris nearly a mile and a half away.

Two of the farm's top stallions — 1957 Derby contenders Bold Ruler and Round Table — were born here on the same day, and Secretariat, sired by Claiborne stallion Bold Ruler and later syndicated for $6.1 million, set a record time of just under two minutes in racing to victory in the 1973 Kentucky Derby, before going on to win the Preakness and Belmont.

Although always glamorous (Queen Elizabeth II famously dined here on a visit to the state), the family has not been without drama.

The current owner, Seth Hancock, got the nod to run the farm following his father's death in 1972 only after the farm's trustees had passed over his older brother, Arthur, for the position because they thought he lacked his younger brother's "seriousness" and astute judgment of horse flesh. Stung, Arthur sold his share of the farm and bought another one, Stone Farm, four miles down the road, where his "lack of seriousness" has been anything but apparent. He owned and bred 1982 Kentucky Derby winner Gato Del Sol and in partnership bred 2000 Derby winner Fusaichi Pegasus. In 1989, one of his horses, Sunday Silence, won the Kentucky

Derby, the Preakness, and the Breeders' Cup Classic.

Claiborne won its own Kentucky Derby in 1984 with the home-bred Swale, who also won the Belmont Stakes before collapsing after a morning bath and dying.

703 Winchester Rd., Paris. (859) 987-2330.
www.clairbornefarm.com

DARBY DAN

Scenic and steeped in history, Old Frankfort Pike has some of the most valuable equine real estate in the world. One of the loveliest locations on the Pike, La Belle, now home to a quartet of small specialty museums affiliated with the Smithsonian, was once the family farm of noted jewelry designer George Headley. Current farms include Donamire and Darby Dan, the latter of which has an illustrious history.

Legendary horseman E.R. Bradley, who assembled breeding stock from around the world, established the original farm, Idle Hour, in 1906. His unfailing ability to select superior horses resulted in four Kentucky Derby winners: Behave Yourself (1921); Bubbling Over (1926); Burgoo King (1932); and Brokers Tip (1933).

John W. Galbreath, a former owner of the Pittsburgh Pirates baseball franchise, bought a portion of Idle Hour after Bradley's death and established his own level of achievement. During his tenure he had two Kentucky Derby winners, Chateaugay (1963) and Proud Clarion (1967); the 1972 English Derby winner (Roberto, named after the Pirates' right fielder Roberto Clemente), and a Breeders' Cup Classic champion (Proud Truth, 1985). Thus, Darby Dan became the only farm in history to win this holy trinity of races.

Today, Galbreath's grandson John Phillips runs the farm, which stands a number of stallions and is home to a select group of Darby Dan mares.

On farm tours, visitors are delighted to get a view of the white-columned mansion, which resembles Tara, Scarlett O'Hara's home in *Gone With the Wind*.

3225 Old Frankfort Pike, Lexington. (859) 254-0424.

www.darbydan.com

DARLEY AT JONABELL FARM

Jonabell's history dates back to 1946 when it was started by noted horse breeder John A. Bell III. During his tenure the farm was home to several important stallions, most notably 1978 Triple Crown winner Affirmed, who is buried in the farm's stallion complex. In 2001 Bell sold the farm to Sheikh Mohammed bin Rashid Al Maktoum of Dubai, who oversees a global breeding operation in six countries and has ties to Fasig-Tipton, the oldest Thoroughbred auction company in the United States.

Jonabell serves as the sheikh's stallion operation; among the prominent stallions standing at stud on the farm are the 2007 Kentucky Derby winner Street Sense and his rival Hard Spun, Bernardini, E Dubai, and Consolidator. It has the distinction of being the only farm with the sires of four Kentucky Derby winners standing at stud at the same time.

Sheikh Mohammed also owns the 2,000-acre Gainsborough Farm on Route 60 in Woodford County, which serves as the broodmare division of his operation, as well as Raceland Farm near Paris, Kentucky.

3333 Bowman Mill Rd., Lexington. (859) 255-8537.

www.darleyamerica.com

GAINESWAY FARM

The story is told in Lexington horse circles that a young man once asked John Gaines, the late owner of Gainesway Farm, how to make $10 million in the Thoroughbred industry. Without batting an eye, Gaines looked at him and said, "Well, son, it's easy. You start off with $20 million and before you know it, you have $10 million!"

Perhaps his joke has some truth to it, but John Gaines was among the most successful of Kentucky's Thoroughbred breeders. His grandfather established the farm, then located off Tates Creek Road, as a Standardbred operation, during which time it bred the winners of every major trotting race in North America, including the Hambletonian twice and the Kentucky Futurity three times — two legs of the trotting Triple Crown. His father, Clarence Gaines, continued the winning tradition while at the same time inventing a nutritionally balanced dog food. By the time John Gaines took over, switched to Thoroughbreds, and the farm moved to its present location, Gainesway saw six of its stallions listed as among the world's leading sires, and Gaines became a racing icon when he created the Breeders' Cup Championship in 1984.

Although the farm encompasses land that was once home to the first Kentucky Derby winner, Aristides (1875), Gainesway's current star attraction is Afleet Alex, who narrowly missed being a Triple Crown winner, emerging victorious in both the 2005 Preakness and Belmont and finishing third in the Derby. His statuesque beauty and winning personality have made him a fan favorite on horse farm tours.

In 1989 Gaines sold Gainesway, which now includes parts of the adjoining Greentree Stud and the C.V. Whitney Farm, to South African tycoon Graham Beck who, in turn, handed over management of the farm to his son Antony. Thoroughbreds are no longer the only attraction on Gainesway's 1,500 prime acres. The farm's gardens have been designated as an arboretum by the American Public Garden Association and serve as a showcase for decorative plants, floral displays, and tree collections, most notably some 45 different kinds of oaks.

<hr>

3750 Paris Pike (US 68), Lexington. (859) 293-2676.
www.gainesway.com

JUDDMONTE FARM

The trophy cases of this farm are filled with gleaming silver, indicating just how successful the farm's owner, Prince Khalid Abdullah of Saudi Arabia, has been in winning important stakes races from Southern California to New York as well as most of the major European races. Although not as high profile as Sheikh Mohammed, the Prince, first cousin to King Abdullah and the brother-in-law of the late ruler, King Fahd, has quietly set about creating a racing and breeding empire, with farms in England and Ireland, as well as the 2,500-acre Lexington property.

From an initial crop of just four yearlings, he has developed one of the world's most successful Thoroughbred empires. Among the top horses in his Kentucky operation (which he started in 1982) are the filly Flute, winner of the 2001 Kentucky Oaks, and the stallions Empire Maker and Mizzen Mast.

Juddmonte's four Eclipse Awards for outstanding breeder are second only to Adena Springs' six.

<hr>

3082 Walnut Hill Rd., Lexington. (859) 272-7629.
www.juddmonte.com

LANE'S END

Although Lane's End actually wasn't founded until 1979 with the purchase of the first 240 acres (it now has 2,000), the land the farm occupies has a long and colorful history. A portion of the land was once occupied by Bosque Bonita (Beautiful Woods) Farm, originally owned by a Confederate general and later by one of Kentucky's leading horsemen. Two of the farm's early horses went on to produce outstanding offspring: Leamington, sire of the first Kentucky Derby winner Aristides, stood at stud here, and Mannie Gray, the dam of 1893 Horse of the Year Domino, was raised on the farm. Currently, Curlin, the 2007 and 2008 Horse of the Year, stands at stud here along with his sire, Smart Strike, and A.P. Indy, a son of 1977 Triple Crown winner Seattle Slew.

The farm's human visitors have been almost as fascinating as its equine stars. In 1875, one year before his disastrous end at the Battle of the Little Big Horn, General George Armstrong Custer came to Bosque Bonita in pursuit of horses for the 7th Cavalry. Another pair of Georges, Presidents George H.W. Bush and George W. Bush, have visited at the invitation of current owner William S. Farish. A former U.S. ambassador to the United Kingdom, Farish

DID YOU KNOW

Those stone fences you see scattered across the Bluegrass region have been a distinctive feature of the area since the 1820s when Irish and Scottish immigrants passed their fence-building knowledge on to slaves and later, free blacks. The fences — unique in that no mortar of any kind was used — remain the most extensive collection of quarried rock fences still standing in the U.S.

has also hosted Her Majesty Queen Elizabeth II of Great Britain, a noted horse lover.

◇◇◇◇ ◇◇◇◇◇◇ ◇◇◇

1500 Midway Rd., Versailles. (859) 873-7300.
www.lanesend.com

SPENDTHRIFT

The late Leslie Combs II, the flamboyant former owner of Spendthrift Farm, liked to joke that the farm got its name after his wife returned from a shopping spree in Europe. A funny story, but not true. The farm was named after Spendthrift, a great stallion owned by one of Combs' ancestors, and the great-grandfather of perhaps the greatest Thoroughbred of all time, Man o' War.

Spendthrift, at 3,000 acres, is one of the world's largest breeders of Thoroughbred racehorses, and during his tenure Leslie Combs was to horse breeding and racing what P.T. Barnum was to the circus — rich, powerful, glamorous, and a born showman. He was the epitome of a gentleman farmer — an astute judge of horseflesh, but with a flair for the dramatic tempered by southern charm and affability.

His lavish parties were the talk of Lexington, and he spared no expense entertaining the rich and powerful, although he self-deprecatingly referred to himself as "Cuzin Leslie."

Spendthrift's horses were able to match the vibrancy of its owner, with some of the greatest Thoroughbreds in racing history calling the farm home: Swaps, Foolish Pleasure, Majestic Prince, Affirmed, and Nashua. The latter, when purchased by Combs in 1955, commanded the highest price ever for a Thoroughbred up to that time — $1,251,200. Combs is generally credited with developing the modern concept of syndication for breeding stallions.

Spendthrift fell on hard times in the 1980s after the Combses sold stock to the public, the Thoroughbred market went through a recession, and the elder Combs died. Today it is owned by B. Wayne Hughes, a California entrepreneur who made his fortune in the storage business.

〰〰〰〰〰〰〰

884 Iron Works Pike, Lexington. (859) 294-0030.
www.spendthriftfarm.com

THREE CHIMNEYS

Started in 1972 on 100 acres and now encompassing 1,500, Three Chimneys is considered to be a model for 21st century Thoroughbred farms. Founder Robert Clay, a descendant of Kentucky's most esteemed statesman, Henry Clay, early on took the unusual step of limiting the number of stallions he accepted. With no more than a dozen stallions, he developed the concept of the "boutique farm," emphasizing quality over quantity.

That quality can be seen in the farm's most famous stallions: Smarty Jones, 2004 Kentucky Derby and Preakness winner; Big Brown, 2008 Derby and Preakness winner; and the most famous of all, the late Seattle Slew, the 1977 Triple Crown winner who stood at stud here for 17 years.

Three Chimneys is divided into three separate areas — one for mares and foals, one for yearlings, and one for stallions. It is one of the most accessible of the area farms, offering several weekly tours by appointment only.

In 2008 the farm got international exposure from an unusual source — as the top fantasy gift in Dallas-based Neiman-Marcus department store's famous Christmas catalog. For $10 million, the lucky purchaser would receive a stable of 12 to 15 Thoroughbreds, complete with stabling, training, and racing for four years. To date, there have been no takers.

Old Frankfort Pike, Midway. (859) 873-7053.

www.threechimneys.com

Other Farms Worth a Look

Note: Most of these farms are not open to the general public, or are open by appointment only, so these are better suggestions for a driving tour of the Bluegrass.

Normandy Farm, 4701 Paris Pike, Lexington. At first sight this beautiful farm on Paris Pike appears more notable for its unusual physical structure — an L-shaped barn (a replica of one in Normandy, France, which provided shelter to then-owner Joseph Widener following a World War I plane crash) with its striking clock tower and ceramic animal figures on cupolas and dormers. But Normandy is also known for its horse cemetery in which Fair Play and Mahubah, sire and dam of Man o' War, are buried at the foot of Fair Play's life-sized statue.

Taylor Made Farm, 2765 Union Mill Rd., Nicholasville. What began as a 120-acre farm for the purpose of caring for mares shipped to Kentucky for breeding has grown to more than 1,600 acres of a multi-pronged Thoroughbred operation. Taylor Made is best known as one of the world's leading sales agencies. Its most triumphant day occurred in 1999 when three of its graduates won Breeders' Cup races, a feat unequaled. The farm is very accommodating to visitors except during breeding season.

Manchester Farm, 2500 Rice Rd., Lexington. Located behind Keeneland Race Course, the 275 acres of the farm are marked by miles of white picket fences and the distinctive blue and white barns with elaborate cupolas and dormers. In winter when it is not hidden by a lush growth of trees, you might be able to catch a glimpse of the farm's white-columned antebellum mansion.

Airdrie Stud, Old Frankfort Pike, Midway. This 2,500-acre property, owned by former Kentucky Governor Brereton Jones and his wife, is part of fabled Woodburn Farm, considered by many to be the birthplace of the American Thoroughbred breeding industry. The farm's beauty is enhanced by the restored Woodburn mansion and the gardens that date back to 1916.

Donamire Farm, Old Frankfort Pike, Lexington. One of the Lexington area's most imposing farms, Donamire belongs to Don and Mira Ball, who have transformed it into a 600-acre showplace that combines a breeding farm and training center. Donamire so impressed Hollywood scouts that it was used for several scenes in the 1999 horse racing thriller *Simpatico*, starring Jeff Bridges and Sharon Stone, and for the 2005 film *Dreamer* starring Kurt Russell and Dakota Fanning. Donamire's gorgeous landscaped grounds can easily be seen from the road.

Adena Springs, 701 Cane Ridge Rd., Paris. Named for the Adena Indians who were attracted to the pure spring water of central Kentucky, the farm moved from its original site in Woodford County to its current 5,000-acre location in Bourbon County in 2005. The farm's owner, Frank Stronach, has amassed an unprecedented number of Breeders' Eclipse Awards — six — and has developed Adena Springs into a state-of-the-art facility.

WinStar Farm, 3001 Pisgah Pike, Midway. The long alley of Osage orange trees lining picturesque rural Pisgah Pike leading up to WinStar promises something special, and the farm doesn't disappoint. Its 1,400 acres include the original 450-acre tract of Silver Pond Farm, settled in the 1700s by a family from Virginia's Tidewater region. The smokehouse, farmhouse, pond, and several of the barns are all original to Silver Pond and are listed on the National Register of Historic Places.

Mill Ridge Farm, 2800 Bowman Mill Rd., Lexington. Perhaps no farm in the Bluegrass has as noble a lineage as this one — both human and equine. Its founder, Alice Headley Chandler, is the daughter of Hal Price Headley, a noted Kentucky horseman and co-founder of Keeneland Race Course, and two of the horses born there, Nicanor and Lentenor, are full brothers to beloved 2006 Kentucky Derby winner Barbaro.

Walmac Farm, 3395 Paris Pike, Lexington. This storied farm was home to three of the most influential stallions of the 20th century — Alleged and Miswaki, both of whom sired more than 100 stakes winners, and Nureyev, who sired more than 100 stakes winners with global earnings totaling $80 million.

Walnut Hall Farm, 3725 Newtown Pike, Lexington. The farm is on property that was originally part of a 9,000-acre land grant given by Patrick Henry in 1770 to his brother-in-law in appreciation for his Revolutionary War service. In 1892 L.V. Harkness purchased 400 of the original acres and developed a respected trotting horse operation. Harkness' original 400 acres have swelled to 5,000, and his great-granddaughter Meg Jewett, the current owner, is carrying on his legacy. Walnut Hall continues as the oldest successful Standardbred horse farm in America.

How to book your horse farm tour

According to the Lexington Convention & Visitors Bureau, there are three ways to get up close (but not too close) and personal with the horses:

* Book a seat on a guided group tour.

* Hire a private guide to take you on a custom-designed tour.

* Call the farm yourself and ask for an appointment.

The one thing you DON'T do is show up at a farm without an appointment and expect to be given a tour. Remember that while many farms are generous in sharing their business with visitors, they are, foremost, businesses and not tourist attractions.

Although tour companies offer horse farm tours daily, reservations are still necessary — preferably made as far in advance as possible as tours tend to sell out, particularly in the spring and summer months. Below is a list of companies specializing in horse farm tours:

Blue Grass Tours (859-252-5744 or 800-755-6956.) Two tours daily Monday through Saturday at 9:00 a.m. and 1:30 p.m.; 1:30 p.m. on Sunday from April through October. Tours last approximately 3 hours and include stops at a local horse farm and Keeneland Race Course as well as other attractions. $30 for adults and $20 for ages 12 and under.

D.W. Guided Tours (859-361-4390.) Narrated van tours are offered year round Monday through Saturday at 9:00 a.m. The tour drives through two farms and other points of interest both horse and non-horse related. Tour lasts about 3 hours and is priced at $25 for adults and $12 for children ages 6 to 12.

Horse Farm Tours, Inc. (859-268-2906 or 800-976-1034.) Year-round daily tours at 9:00 a.m. and 1:00 p.m. Every tour includes a drive through historic downtown, a drive past Calumet, two horse farms, Keeneland, and Thoroughbred Park. Tours last 3 hours and depart from several area hotels. $32 for adults and $22 for children under 12.

Thoroughbred Heritage Tours (859-260-8687 or 800-808-9533.) Tours are offered daily at 9:00 a.m. and 1:15 p.m. from the downtown Lexington Center and several hotels. A 3-hour tour, it includes a drive past Calumet Farm, a tour of Keeneland, a top breeding complex, and several other points of interest. Adults, $28; children 12 and under, $16.

Unique Horse Farm Tours (859-233-4303 or 800-678-8813.) Departing from the Kentucky Horse Park twice daily, this 2 1/2 hour tour gives a "behind-the-scenes" look at what makes Lexington the Horse Capital of the World. Adults, $25; children 12 and under, $15.

Suburban Woman's Club Monthly Horse Farm Tours (859-624-2338.) This local club has more than three decades of experience conducting horse farm tours. Tours, which begin at 10:00 a.m. and last 4 hours, feature a knowledgeable guide with connections at local farms plus lunch. $50 inclusive. Call for applicable tour dates.

Note: On individual tours, it is customary to tip the groom who shows you around the farm between $5 and $10. On private and/or guided tours the tip may or may not be included so it is always best to ask.

Customized Tours

If you want to see specific farms and want to set your own pace, you can arrange a personalized tour using a private guide. These tour companies often have access to farms not open to groups or individuals, and you can stop and go as you please. In most cases, these companies provide "step-on" guides who join you in your vehicle, but some provide their own transport.

Customized tours are obviously more expensive (from $75 to $150 depending on length, content, number of people in the party, use of vehicle, and tour company selected). Some of the companies offering customized tours are:

Blue Grass Tours 859-252-5744

Tours of Tradition by Scott Goodlett Inc. 859-879-0319

800-450-6444

Unbridled Horse Tours 859-255-7863; 859-333-8940

Kentucky Horse Tours 859-312-1124

Horses of Kentucky 859-277-4625

Lexington in Touch Inc. 859-224-4226

John Midbo 859-278-9488

Karen Edelstein, private guide 859-266-5465

Lexington Connection, Inc. 859-269-4040

Kentucky Living History Tours 859-293-9367

4

Race Courses

"And God took a handful of southerly wind, blew His breath upon it, and created the horse."

— BEDOUIN LEGEND

The best place to see Thoroughbreds do what they do best is at one of Kentucky's world-famous race-tracks, although you have to time your visit appropriately if you have specific tracks and/or meets in mind. Keeneland Race Course in Lexington has only two three-week race meets a year — in April and October — while Churchill Downs in Louisville, in addition to being the site of the Kentucky Derby the first Saturday of every May, has a full card of Thoroughbred racing from April to mid-July (spring meet) and for three weeks in November (fall meet).

CHURCHILL DOWNS, LOUISVILLE
HISTORY

The twin spires rise from the Louisville landscape — beacons summoning the faithful to Thoroughbred racing's most hallowed spot. It is no exaggeration to say that few other sports venues are as recognized around the world as Churchill Downs.

While horse racing in Kentucky dates back to 1789, the sport's legendary locale wasn't to open until nearly a century later in 1875. Zealous owners were still racing their prize Thoroughbreds on downtown streets when Colonel M. Lewis Clark, grandson of the explorer William Clark (see Chapter 2), decided to give Louisville and the industry the racecourse they deserved. Encountering some initial opposition from a rival group of horsemen, Clark persevered, and his new track, Churchill Downs (named for his uncles John and Henry Churchill who had leased him the 80 acres), opened in May 1875. His inaugural race meet featured three major stakes races — the Kentucky Derby, Kentucky Oaks, and Clark Handicap — fashioned after three of England's premier races — the Epsom Derby, Epsom Oaks, and St. Leger Stakes.

While the Oaks, held the day before the Derby, remains a prestigious race for three-year-old fillies, and the Clark has been moved to the fall meet schedule, it was the Kentucky Derby that quickly took its place among the world's most iconic sporting events — often referred to as "the most exciting two minutes in sports." Over its long history the Kentucky Derby has become the first and brightest jewel of Thoroughbred racing's Triple Crown, and there is no more perfect setting for this jewel than Churchill Downs.

THE RUN FOR THE ROSES

Picture, if you will, a day full of sunshine (hopefully) and high spirits (definitely) — the first Saturday in May. Men resembling GQ models and women in hats that would have made Coco Chanel envious sip mint juleps. On Millionaires' Row the world's rich and famous congregate, while in the infield a more casually dressed (or undressed) crowd, including a large contingent of college students, doesn't really care that they will probably never see the finish line. On this day the aristocracy and the bourgeoisie, those with deep pocketbooks and the two-dollar bettors, those who have meticulously studied the bloodlines of the horses and those who pick their horses because they like the names — are all part of the same family.

DID YOU KNOW

Man o' War, generally considered the greatest
of all Thoroughbreds, never raced in the Kentucky
Derby. In fact, he never raced in the state of Kentucky.

When the melodious strains of "My Old Kentucky Home" begin, people who have never set foot in the commonwealth get tears in their eyes and lumps in their throats. Churchill Downs becomes the center of the universe, and the ghosts of the greats that have thundered down the backstretch — Whirlaway, Citation, Northern Dancer, Secretariat, Seattle Slew, Genuine Risk, and Barbaro, among them — are all there at the finish line. This is the Run for the Roses, and for two minutes it doesn't get any better than this.

FAMOUS NAMES (AND NOT JUST THE HORSES)

With all the hoopla surrounding the Derby, it's little wonder the race has attracted the world's most famous names — human as well as equine — to Churchill Downs on that first Saturday in May. Over the years celebrities have become a Derby staple. Pick a year — any year — and it's a safe bet that celebs, hats on head and juleps in hand, will be doing the red carpet thing.

In 1937 Babe Ruth and J. Edgar Hoover watched as War Admiral (who was to go on to win the Triple Crown) crossed the finish line first. In 1969 President and Mrs. Richard Nixon saw Majestic Prince claim the title. In 1974 Princess Margaret, Bob Hope, and David Brinkley cheered on Cannonade; in 1999 Muhammad Ali, Donald Trump, Al and Tipper Gore, and Rush Limbaugh were among those who saw Charismatic race to victory; and in 2007 the horses were almost eclipsed by the presence of no less a personage than England's Queen Elizabeth II, accompanied by Prince Philip and Lane's End Farm owner William Farish.

CHURCHILL FUN FACTS

- Kentucky is clearly the birthplace of choice for Derby winners, with 15 times the number of winners as the next closest state, Florida.
- Two Canadian-bred horses, Northern Dancer (1964) and Sunny's Halo (1983), and two English-bred horses, Omar Khayyam (1917) and Tomy Lee (1959), have won the Derby.
- If you are looking for a Derby winner that was a high-priced sale yearling, hold on to your wallet. To date, only three winners have cost $500,000 or more in the auction ring. The 2000 winner, Fusaichi Pegasus, was the most expensive, going for $4 million. Consecutive Derby winners, Alysheba (1987) and Winning Colors (1988), went for $500,000 and $575,000, respectively.
- If you have a horse in the Derby, you probably will want him/her to have the Number 1 or Number 5 post, as those have been the most consistently successful, with 12 winners each breaking out of those gates.
- The winning horse is presented with a blanket of 554 red roses after the race.
- More than 120,000 mint juleps are served at the track each year on Derby day.

Other celebrated attendees over the years have included royalty — the Duke and Duchess of Windsor, Prince Ranier, and Prince Albert of Monaco; politicians — George H.W. Bush and George W. Bush; Hollywood celebrities — John Wayne, Lana Turner, Sylvester Stallone, Jessica Simpson; sports figures — Serena Williams, Joe Namath and Dick Vitale; and other notables ranging from Lee Iaccoca to General Norman Schwarzkopf.

Still, on Derby day the celebrities, politicians, royalty, and captains of industry play second fiddle to the real stars — the horses.

BUILDING FOR THE FUTURE

Churchill Downs was named a National Historic Landmark in 1986. It has a seating capacity of 51,000, although on Derby day, standing room only admission to the infield and paddocks area can cause attendance to swell to nearly 165,000. Colonel Clark might be hard put to recognize his track today. In 2005, Churchill Downs completed a four-year, $121 million renovation, replacing the clubhouse, adding 79 new luxury suites, and refurbishing the spires.

Today, those newly gleaming spires remain a tribute to Clark's vision.

Visitors to the commonwealth don't have to brave the Derby day crowds to enjoy all that Churchill Downs has to offer. As previously mentioned, post-Derby racing continues through mid-July, with a fall racing card in November, and it broadcasts year-round live simulcasts from tracks across America. In addition, Churchill Downs routinely plays host to the Breeders' Cup, racing's championship day. The fall 2010 event will mark the seventh time the championship has been held at the Louisville track.

Churchill Downs is also the site of the outstanding Kentucky Derby Museum (see separate entry in Chapter 5).

700 Central Ave., Louisville. (502) 636-4400.
www.churchilldowns.com.

KEENELAND RACE COURSE, LEXINGTON

Listed on the National Register of Historic Places, Keeneland Race Course has been considered one of Kentucky's pre-eminent tracks since it opened in 1936. It is certainly considered by many to be the most beautiful, with its imposing tree-lined drive leading to the stone clubhouse; the elegant paddock area; and manicured grounds dotted with pink redbuds and white dogwoods during the spring meet and a kaleidoscope of colors during the fall meet. Most agree that this is Thoroughbred racing at its best. (Keeneland's long-standing mantra is "racing as it was meant to be.")

Tradition is everything at Keeneland: The dress code, the pre-race parade of horses in the paddock, the sea of binoculars raised at precisely the right moment. Up until the 1990s, the track eschewed the use of a public address system, believing, as did many of Lexington's racing gentry, that if you knew your racing silks, there was no need for amplified announcements. (Actually, the lack of a public address system did not result from aesthetics but the track's nearly going broke during the Great Depression.) Keeneland finally came into the electronic age in 1997 when it hired its first race caller.

On its nearly 1,000-acre complex, there are — in addition to the main track — a training track; sales pavilion; 57 barns capable of housing 1,951 horses; the clubhouse; library; gift shop; the Keene mansion; and the legendary Keeneland Track Kitchen.

Keeneland has two live race meets — the spring meet (three weeks in April) highlighted by the prestigious Toyota Blue Grass Stakes, often an indicator of which horses will fare well in the Derby, and the fall meet (three weeks in October). On the fall racing card is a series of races leading up to the Breeders' Cup World Championships held every fall.

Speaking of the Derby, Keeneland hosts what has to be the world's biggest Derby bash outside of Churchill Downs. On the first Saturday in May, some 20,000 racing fans take over the grounds, from the paddock to the grandstand to the corporate boxes to celebrate Derby day in true Kentucky fashion.

Keeneland is open year-round for training, and visitors can enjoy a railside view of Thoroughbreds getting their morning exercise (between 6:00 a.m. and 10:00 a.m.) and then take a stroll through the barns afterward. Unlike most other tracks, the Keene-

DID YOU KNOW

The only horse ever to defeat Man o' War was named — appropriately — Upset.

land barns are not off limits to the public though visitors should keep their distance from sometimes-fractious racehorses.

KEENELAND HORSE SALES

Keeneland is the largest and most prestigious Thoroughbred auction company in the world. With close to $1 billion in annual sales, it is the global marketplace for Thoroughbreds.

Since its sales began in 1943, Keeneland has sold more champions and stakes winners than any other sale company. A list of its graduates includes Kentucky Derby winners Big Brown, War Emblem, Fusaichi Pegasus, Real Quiet, Thunder Gulch, Sunday Silence, Winning Colors, Alysheba, Spectacular Bid, and Hoop Jr., who sold at the very first yearling sale.

Keeneland has four sales annually, with the September Yearling Sale and the November Breeding Stock Sale attracting deep pockets from around the world. If you want to know how deep, just check out the lineup of private planes at Blue Grass Airport across Versailles Road from Keeneland. However, a better indicator is that Keeneland can claim record prices for yearlings ($13.1 million for Seattle Dancer, a son of English Triple Crown winner Nijinsky II), broodmare prospects ($9 million for Ashado), and pregnant broodmares ($7 million for the appropriately named Cash Run).

The sales are open to the public; visitors may attend the auctions free of charge and without making a reservation; just be sure you don't twitch your nose or scratch your ear unless you're serious about buying a Thoroughbred.

KEENELAND TRACK KITCHEN

Inside a small building tucked away near Keeneland's stable areas, the walls are lined with photos of such equine stars as Strike the Gold, Swale, Alydar, Risen Star, and Gato Del Sol. A Lexington landmark since 1936, the Keeneland Track Kitchen has been the place where owners, trainers, exercise riders, and track employees rub elbows over early morning coffee before heading off to the barn or the track or the executive boardroom (the Track Kitchen is nothing if not egalitarian).

It's a place where the general public can feel part of the rarefied world of Thoroughbred racing for five bucks — the cost of a bountiful breakfast of eggs, bacon, sausage, biscuits and gravy, Belgian waffles, baked apples, and grits.

Wizened exercise riders, weighing no more than supermodels, tear into breakfasts that would do justice to a lumberjack. At a table near a window, a group of people may sit in jovial companionship, debating the odds on the filly in the fourth, while at a corner table, a solitary man pores over a *Daily Racing Form.*

In short, this is quite a scene, and short of owning your own Thoroughbred, the best place in the Bluegrass to get up close and personal with the horse crowd.

The Track Kitchen is open to the public for breakfast (6:00 a.m.–9:00 a.m.) daily except for certain holidays, and the first two weeks in February when it closes. It is open for lunch (11:00 a.m.–5:00 p.m.) during races and sales. (859) 288-4147.

KEENE PLACE

George Washington may not have slept here, but his friend, the Marquis de Lafayette, did.

Visitors traveling along Versailles Road pass an imposing columned mansion just before reaching the entrance to Keeneland. They may just assume it is another of the grand homes located on area horse farms.

But this particular grand home has a heap of history embedded in its walls. Built in 1805 by the Keene family, it was the site

SOME INTERESTING KEENELAND FACTS

- There is no maximum bet at Keeneland; you can bet $1 million (or more). However, you need to have the cash at the window or the credit line on the self-betting machine to make that gargantuan wager.

- During World War II, Keeneland held its spring races at Churchill Downs. In the years of that conflict, Keeneland was considered a "suburban plant" (being six miles from downtown Lexington), and was requested not to open due to the related shortage of rubber, and transportation issues. As a result, the track leased facilities at Churchill Downs and held its spring meets there from 1943 to 1945.

- Although Keeneland is now internationally known for its yearling sales held every September, its first yearling sale, in 1943, was conducted not by Keeneland personnel but by Fasig-Tipton, a rival sales company. Prior to this, Kentucky breeders would ship their horses to upstate New York where those wealthy enough to buy them spent their summers around the track at Saratoga. However, the success of Keeneland's first yearling sale — held under a tent in the paddock area — was enough to convince Kentucky horsemen to hold an annual event in their own backyard.

- The laurel wreath with the KA insignia on the Keeneland gateposts does not stand for Keeneland Association as many think, but rather for the Kentucky Association track. It was the identifying logo for the oldest continually operating track in North America when it closed in 1933. Hal Price Headley, Keeneland's first president, is credited with spotting the symbol and telling workers to "grab those gateposts."

- Keeneland serves more than 250 gallons of burgoo each race day. This typical Kentucky dish — a hearty stew made of several different types of meat — allegedly is the recipe of the one-time manager of Idle Hour Farm, Jim Looney, whose delicious dish earned him the nickname Burgoo King. Colonel E.R. Bradley, the farm's owner, also gave the sobriquet to one of his colts. The human Burgoo King continued ladling out bowls of his famous stew, while his equine counterpart won the 1932 Kentucky Derby.

of a visit in 1825 by the Marquis de Lafayette who had offered his considerable military skills to George Washington during the Revolutionary War. Lafayette's visit is commemorated on a historic marker on Versailles Road, and Lexington's county is named Fayette in his honor.

The mansion's more recent history is dominated by the larger-than-life horseman, John O. "Jack" Keene. In 1935 he sold his stud farm to the Keeneland Association, which opened Keeneland Race Course the next year.

The house remained the property of the Keene family, although entirely surrounded by land now owned by Keeneland. In 2003 the Keeneland Association purchased the remaining 15 acres, including the house, and embarked on a six-year restoration project.

Keene Place is open only for private functions and thus not accessible to the general public, but the restoration of this "Bluegrass gem" has returned the mansion to the place in history that it richly deserves.

4201 Versailles Rd., Lexington. (859-254-3412). www.keeneland.com. Free self-guided walking tours of Keeneland's grandstand begin at the clubhouse adjacent to the grandstand south entrance. A brochure with a tour map can be picked up at the gift shop.

ELLIS PARK, HENDERSON

Its twin spires may not be as famous as those of Churchill Downs, but western Kentucky's Ellis Park in Henderson has a history nearly as colorful. Built in 1922 by the Green River Jockey Club, which hoped to model it after New York's famed Saratoga, the track began its existence with a design snafu and an opening race featuring the wrong breed of horse.

The owners, wanting it to be one of the nation's longest tracks, specified the length to be one-and-a-half miles, but the architect submitted a plan that made it three-eighths of a mile shorter. As a result of a time crunch, the shorter track was approved. While always planned as a Thoroughbred track, Standardbreds, or trotting horses, were featured at the park's opening meet in October 1922, and it wasn't until a month later that the first

Thoroughbred race was held.

Over its long history Ellis Park has seen its share of thrills and more than its share of hard times (financial woes leading to the founders' bankruptcy, the 1937 flooding of the Ohio River that saw the waters reach the mezzanine level of the grandstand, and a November 2005 tornado that damaged the physical plant).

Ellis Park conducts live racing beginning in early July and continuing through Labor Day, and year-round simulcast wagering.

3300 US Highway 41 N., Henderson. (270) 826-0608. www.ellisparkracing.com.

TURFWAY PARK, FLORENCE

Called Latonia Race Course when it opened in 1959, this northern Kentucky track was located just a few miles south of the original Latonia, which hosted Thoroughbred racing from 1883 until its demise in 1939. In its heyday, the Latonia Derby rivaled the Kentucky Derby in prestige and many of the same horses ran in both races.

Today Turfway is partly owned by Keeneland and hosts two major events — the Lane's End Stakes in March, a prep for the Kentucky Derby, and the Kentucky Cup Day of Champions in September, a prep for the Breeders' Cup World Championships. In 2005 Turfway became the first track in North America to install Polytrack, an all-weather racing surface deemed safer for horses and riders. The track, which holds more live race dates than any other Kentucky track, offers three meets a year — fall, holiday, and winter/spring meets as well as simulcast wagering year round.

7500 Turfway Rd., Florence. (859) 371-0200 or (859) 647-4705. www.turfway.com.

THE RED MILE, LEXINGTON

The second-oldest harness racing track in the United States, The Red Mile gets its name from the obvious — a surface of rich red clay measuring one mile in length. For nearly a century and a half the track has been host to the elite of the Standardbred industry, but it had a less than auspicious beginning.

It was just a few months after Aristides won the first Kentucky Derby that the Kentucky Trotting Horse Breeders Association decided it was not to be outdone by its counterparts in the Thoroughbred industry. Thus, on September 28, 1875, the organization inaugurated its state-of-the-art facilities and was sorely disappointed when just a few diehards showed up to christen it. The reason was quickly discovered: The organizers had failed to advertise the grand opening. That was quickly remedied for the next race and The Red Mile became an instant success.

Recognized as the world's fastest harness track, it has generated more two-minute-mile world champions and record holders than any other Standardbred track and is the site every September of the Kentucky Futurity, the third leg of the Triple Crown for Standardbreds.

Visitors are often curious about the unusual Round Barn that dominates the entrance to the track. The octagonal structure, listed on the National Register of Historic Places, originally housed floral exhibits and later served a barn, but is now used for private events. Another historic building adjacent to The Red Mile houses the sales pavilion of Tattersalls, the renowned international horse sales organization.

1200 Red Mile Rd., Lexington. (859) 255-0752.
www.theredmile.com.

5

Horse Attractions

"There is something about the outside of a horse that is good for the inside of a man."

— WINSTON CHURCHILL

Sir Winston's sentiment is echoed throughout the Bluegrass. Horses, in common with the area's other two passions — bourbon and basketball — can be indeed good for the inside of a man. They are certainly good for the commonwealth's tourism. From a smattering of first-class museums to the final resting place of famous Thoroughbreds to the only park in the world dedicated to the horse, the noble steed is a Kentucky tourism superstar.

KENTUCKY HORSE PARK

He stands there, forever frozen in bronze — the most gallant Thoroughbred in the history of racing — welcoming all to his kingdom. He is Man o' War, and his statue towers above the cemetery where he is buried, along with his most famous offspring, Triple Crown winner War Admiral. His kingdom is the 1,200 acres of rolling bluegrass that make up the Kentucky Horse Park, the only park of its kind in the world.

If the commonwealth has an ambassador to the world, it is surely the horse, and here the world can visit him on his own turf. On land that was once part of Walnut Hall Standardbred farm, the Horse Park has emerged as one of the world's most unique attractions — a working horse farm, educational theme park, and equine competition facility dedicated to man's 50-million-year-long love affair with the horse.

The idea of the Horse Park, however, almost soured before it began. If Alaska was once derogatorily referred to as "Seward's Folly," the Horse Park was considered to be "Brown's Folly" (referring to then-Governor John Y. Brown, who lobbied for the park in the 1970s at the behest of Thoroughbred breeder and visionary John R. Gaines). Many spoke out against the project from the beginning, saying that it would be an expensive flop and a waste of taxpayers' money. Brown, with the clairvoyant powers of Karnak the Magician, soldiered on and ultimately proved to the naysayers that he knew what he was talking about. Today the Horse Park attracts in the neighborhood of one million visitors annually.

The magic begins with Man o' War's statue at the entrance to the park. The legendary stallion, nicknamed "Big Red" during his racing career, won 20 of 21 races, breaking old records and setting new ones. "Watching him run," wrote one sportswriter, "was like watching a living flame go down the track."

After retiring from racing, he came back to Kentucky, where during his 27-year stud career he sired 379 named foals, most notably War Admiral. When he died in 1947, his body lay in state for three days, allowing 2,000 sorrowful racing fans to pay their last respects.

But Man o' War is only one of the Thoroughbred giants honored at the park. Just to the right of the visitor's center is another magnificent statue — this one of 1973 Triple Crown winner Secretariat, who, half a century after Man o' War, also became known to his legion of fans as "Big Red."

Lest one get the idea that all the park's stars are in bronze, a visit to the Hall of Champions will prove otherwise. Inside one barn resides one of the leading money-winning Thoroughbreds of all time, Cigar (another, John Henry, lived here until his death in 2007), a Kentucky Derby winner, Funny Cide, and a Standardbred Triple Crown winner, Western Dreamer, as well as champion Saddlebred and Quarter horses. Several times a day, from March 15 to October 31, they are brought out from the barn to meet their adoring fans.

While prize-winning Thoroughbreds are the horses most associated with Kentucky, they are only one of many breeds represented at the Horse Park. Some 53 different breeds — from the enormous English Shire to the dainty Spanish Paso Fino, from the Appaloosa beloved by the Indians to the stately Arabian, beloved by the desert sheikhs — call the park home. You can make their acquaintance at the twice-daily Parade of Breeds, a real crowd pleaser (March through October).

At the International Museum of the Horse (see separate entry), you can see permanent and traveling equine art exhibitions; at the American Saddlebred Museum (see separate entry), you can learn all about Kentucky's oldest native breed, and by watching the film *Thou Shalt Fly Without Wings*, at the visitor's center you can see why man's passion for horses continues unabated.

Some of the park's self-guided activities and features include farrier and tack shops, historic barns, and more than 30 miles of the Bluegrass region's distinctive white-plank fences. Children are sure to love the horse-drawn carriage tours and pony rides. The park also offers escorted trail rides.

For campers, the park offers a full-service 260-site campground, with bathhouses, grocery store, gift shop, fire rings, picnic tables, and facilities for leisure activities.

In addition to the daily activities, the Kentucky Horse Park is also home to many seasonal events including polo, steeplechase, and the annual Kentucky Rolex Three-Day Event, an Olympic-level triathlon (dressage, cross-country, and show jumping) for horses and riders. Horse shows for a variety of disciplines take place every weekend from early spring to late fall and include prestigious Grand Prix jumping competitions.

In 2010 the Kentucky Horse Park will host its largest event ever when the Alltech FEI World Equestrian Games come to Lexington, marking the first time the Games have been held outside of Europe.

4089 Iron Works Pkwy., Lexington, 40511, off I-75 at exit 120. (800) 678-8813 or (859) 233-4303. www.kyhorsepark.com. In summer, the park is open 7 days a week, 9:00 a.m.–5:00 p.m.; check for winter hours and openings.
Admission: adults, $14; children, $7; under 6, free (includes admission to park events and museums).

Horse Museums

INTERNATIONAL MUSEUM OF THE HORSE, LEXINGTON

Located on the grounds of the Kentucky Horse Park, this affiliate of the Smithsonian is the largest equestrian museum in the world. Within its 38,000 square feet of space are exhibitions and displays featuring some 100 different breeds. The museum's central exhibition, "The Legacy of the Horse," documents man's more than 50-million-year relationship with the horse.

Other attractions include the Calumet Farm Collection, which serves as a showcase for the fabled farm's impressive array of racing trophies, and the newest exhibit, "Affirmed: The Making of a Champion," which opened in 2007. Over the years, the museum has also hosted temporary international exhibitions, most notably "Imperial China: The Art of the Horse in Chinese History," and

"All the Queen's Horses: The Role of the Horse in British History," which drew no less a personage to its opening than Great Britain's Princess Anne, who, like her mother, is a keen equestrian.

4089 Iron Works Pkwy., Lexington. (859) 233-4303.

www.imh.org.

AMERICAN SADDLEBRED MUSEUM, LEXINGTON

Also located at the Horse Park, the American Saddlebred Museum is dedicated to Kentucky's only native breed. Featuring both permanent and changing exhibitions, the museum traces the history and heritage of the breed through the largest collection of Saddlebred artifacts in the world, as well as in photographs and fine art.

The lovely statue striking a trotting pose in front of the museum is that of Supreme Sultan, the sire of many champion Saddlebreds.

4083 Iron Works Pkwy., Lexington. (859) 259-2746.

www.asbmuseum.org.

KENTUCKY DERBY MUSEUM, LOUISVILLE

Just outside Gate 1 at storied Churchill Downs and housed in a white, two-story Georgian structure is one of the commonwealth's most fascinating museums. The tone is set by a 360-degree high-definition video presentation that places visitors square in the middle of flying hooves and scattering dirt during "The Great Race." Nearly 100 projectors throw images around the huge oval of the museum Great Hall in a breathtaking kaleidoscope that replicates the Derby's unique excitement. It just gets better after that.

Over two floors of interactive exhibits, visitors immerse themselves in the "Sport of Kings." One of the most entertaining exhibits is the Derby Time Machine, which, via newsreels, allows visitors to view past Derby races. Just push a button and key in a year, and they're off and running. You can watch War Admiral, Man o' War's most famous offspring, take the first leg of the 1937 Triple Crown, or see Secretariat set a track record of 1:59 2/5 in winning the 1973 Derby, en route to his own Triple Crown.

A guaranteed kids' favorite is the "Riders Up" exhibit which teaches them how to ride like a jockey. The museum also offers a resident Thoroughbred and Miniature Horse exhibit as well as guided walking tours of Churchill Downs' barns and backside (did you know the backside has its own mayor?), and private tours that will take you into famed Millionaires' Row.

During the racing season, the museum is home to former Kentucky Derby contenders Perfect Drift (2002) and Phantom on Tour (1992). Visitors can meet them in the stable next to the museum.

◇◇◇ ◇◇◇◇ ◇◇◇ ◇◇◇◇

704 Central Ave., Louisville. (502) 637-1111. www.derbymuseum. org. Monday–Saturday, 9:00 a.m–5:00 p.m. and Sunday, 11:00 a.m–5:00 p.m. (Closed on Thanksgiving and Christmas as well as

Derby and Oaks days — the first Friday and Saturday in May).
Tours of Churchill Downs, which must be booked through the
museum, are offered from March 15–Nov. 30, excluding Derby and
Oaks days. General admission: adults, $12; seniors,
$11; students, $8; children 5–12, $5; under 5, free.

◇◇◇◇◇◇◇◇◇◇◇◇◇◇

A one-and-a-half hour "Behind the Scenes" tour, which gives
visitors exclusive access to VIP areas such as jockeys' quarters
and Millionaires' Row is offered year round, except for race days.
(Monday–Saturday at 10 a.m., 12 noon, and 2 p.m. and
Sundays at 12:30 and 2:30 p.m.)
There is an additional $10 charge for this tour.

Other Horse Attractions

OLD FRIENDS AT DREAM CHASE FARM

Old Friends retirement home is similar to many others. Some of
the senior citizens can occasionally get grumpy and out-of-sorts.
All are past their physical prime — their knees have long since
given way to arthritis, their once-muscular bodies show the rav-
ages of age, and one has even lost an eye.

Still, like most of those living in retirement communities, these
old-timers welcome visitors, but unlike most, they seem uninter-
ested in long conversations, preferring instead to nibble on a carrot stick or a sugar cube the visitor might be inclined to offer.

The farm, 52 acres of rolling Bluegrass farmland just outside of
Georgetown in Scott County, has become the nation's first retirement community for Thoroughbreds, a safe haven where they can
live out their lives once their racing and breeding careers are over.
Started by Michael Blowen, a former movie critic for *The Boston*

Globe and a passionate horse lover, and his wife, Diane White, a former *Globe* columnist, Old Friends is home to between 25 and 30 horses at any given time — some of whose careers were legendary and some whose careers proved to be less than stellar. It doesn't matter to Blowen and White; to them, all Thoroughbreds deserve a happy home.

That seems to be the philosophy of all concerned with the project. Many of the horses have been donated by their former owners; veterinarians donate their services to provide for the horses' health care, and volunteers show visitors around the farm. Visitors, in turn, can help support Old Friends by purchasing a share in one of the horses (from $25 to $100).

1841 Paynes Depot Rd., Georgetown. (502) 863-1775. www. oldfriendsequine.org. Free daily tours; reservations required.

HORSE CEMETERIES

Horse cemeteries are a Bluegrass tradition dating back to 1875 when a monument was erected to mark the grave of the great stallion Lexington. Don't expect to find it, however, as Lexington's remains were exhumed shortly after his burial and donated to the Smithsonian Institution. (At press time, there were plans underfoot to bring those remains back to the Bluegrass.)

Still, there is no dearth of Thoroughbred memorials — some 400 throughout the Bluegrass region — most of them located in cemeteries on the farms that were home to these great horses.

Darby Dan, one of the more accessible of the area farms, has a lovely cemetery in which are buried a number of great horses, including Black Toney, the patriarch of the original Idle Hour Farm, and the legendary stallions Graustark and Roberto.

The cemetery at Calumet Farm has the graves of four Kentucky

Derby winners, Citation, Pensive, Ponder, and Tim Tam, as well as that of Alydar, the magnificent stallion credited with returning Calumet to its glory days.

Claiborne Farm found that one cemetery wasn't enough to contain the remains of the impressive stallions and mares that have had a connection to the farm. The main cemetery, behind the farm office, has a pillared entrance that leads to the graves of some of the greatest horses in history: Nasrullah, Buckpasser, Hoist the Flag, Round Table, Bold Ruler, Gallant Fox, Mr. Prospector, and Secretariat. The second cemetery is the burial place of other stallions and mares.

Other area farms with notable horse cemeteries include Spendthrift, Normandy, Lane's End, Stoner Creek Stud, Walmac, Overbrook, and Three Chimneys.

Not all of these cemeteries are open to the public, but the most famous horse grave is available for all to see. Man o' War is buried at the Kentucky Horse Park in a lovely plot alongside his two most famous offspring, Triple Crown winner War Admiral and War Relic. Man o' War originally was buried at Faraway Farm, but with the completion of the Horse Park in 1978, the grave was moved to its current site where it rests beneath a life-sized statue of the horse once described as radiating majesty, energy, and power — "a veritable Alexander awaiting new worlds to conquer."

THOROUGHBRED TRAINING CENTER

If you are looking for a real "behind-the-scenes" tour that will show you Thoroughbreds at work and at rest, look no further than the Thoroughbred Training Center. Located in the midst of lush horse farms on Paris Pike, the center, owned by the Keeneland Association, encompasses 240 acres of rolling Bluegrass terrain and generally stables anywhere from 900 to 1,000 horses.

The training center provides the perfect venue for the novice horse lover to see up close and personal all the attention and hard work that go into taking an untested horse and making him/her into a champion. On guided tours that last from an hour to an hour-and-a-half, visitors have a chance to see horses during their morning workouts on one of the center's two tracks, observe top-notch trainers as they work with potential future champions, and tour the barns and paddocks where the horses spend their "off-duty" time.

⬦⬦⬦⬦⬦⬦⬦⬦⬦⬦⬦⬦⬦

3380 Paris Pike, Lexington. (859) 293-1853. www.thethoroughbredcenter.com. Tours are available Monday–Saturday at 9:00 a.m. (April–October) and Monday–Friday at 9:00 a.m. (November–March) and by appointment.

THOROUGHBRED PARK, LEXINGTON

First-time visitors to Lexington are often shocked to see what appears to be a horse race in progress on the downtown's Main Street. They are even more shocked to discover that these seven magnificent horses are made not of skin, bone, muscle, and sinew but of bronze. Thoroughbred Park is a lovely, compact 2.5-acre oasis at the east end of Main Street dedicated to the giants of the industry.

In one corner is a beautiful garden of red roses (floral symbol of the Kentucky Derby) that bloom from late spring throughout the summer, while around the perimeter are plaques commemorating individuals who have left their mark in the Thoroughbred industry — a breeding and racing walk of fame.

The park's biggest draw is the statues — the racing horses juxtaposed against a pastoral scene of mares and foals idling in a pasture. It makes a perfect spot for a respite from touring, and

always seems to attract photographers angling for the best shot.
The bronze horse theme is continued a few blocks down Main
Street with the stylized statue of a prancing horse — a gift from
the People's Republic of China on the occasion of the Kentucky
Horse Park's exhibition, "Imperial China."

**Intersection of Main Street and Midland Avenue in downtown
Lexington.**

JUNIOR LEAGUE HORSE SHOW OF LEXINGTON

Held every July at Lexington's Red Mile racetrack, the Junior
League Show is the world's largest outdoor Saddlebred horse
show and the first leg of the American Saddlebred Triple Crown.
It annually attracts some 30,000 spectators and 1,000 exhibitors
from around the world who compete for prize money in events
ranging from pleasure driving to showing three- and five-gaited
saddle horses.

**General admission is $5 Monday–Thursday; $10 Friday and Sat-
urday. Reserved seating in grandstands is $8 Monday–Thursday;
$15 Friday and Saturday. A limited number of boxes (6 seats) are
available starting at $295, which includes tickets for all show ses-
sions. For ticket information, go to www.lexjrleague.com.**

MERCER COUNTY FAIR & HORSE SHOW

Established in 1828, the Mercer County Fair & Horse Show is the longest running event of its type in the country, with even the Civil War and World Wars I and II unable to disrupt one of Harrodsburg's signature attractions.

Its modest beginning served as a way for the citizens to trade horses, even then the lifeblood of the region. In later years it allowed a similar swapping of other forms of livestock; still later, a midway appeared, heralding a carnival whose attractions have evolved from the once naughty "hootchy-kootchy show" to the Facebook generation's favorite ride, the gravity defying Cobra.

While the midway attracts the locals, the horse show featuring competitions between top Saddlebreds appeals to a wider audience — hundreds of competitors from dozens of states, including actor William Shatner, who has a Saddlebred farm in the Bluegrass and is a loyal fan of the event.

The Mercer Fair & Horse Show is held every July.
P.O. Box 444, Harrodsburg.
www.mercerfair.com.

KENTUCKY STATE FAIR WORLD'S CHAMPIONSHIP HORSE SHOW

The World's Championship, held in Louisville every August in conjunction with the Kentucky State Fair, is one of the most prestigious shows of its type in the country. It attracts riders from around the world with more than 2,000 trotting horses competing for $1 million in prize money. Each year, world champion Saddlebreds are crowned in a number of competition categories.

The championship has been held every year since its founding in 1902, except for in 1904, when no fair was held, and in 1945, when the fair was canceled due to World War II. The event is one of the three horse shows that compose the Saddlebred "Triple Crown," in addition to the Junior League Horse Show in Lexington and the American Royal in Kansas City, Missouri.

Kentucky Exposition Center, 937 Phillips La., Louisville. For ticket information, call (502) 367-5000 or visit ww.kystatefair.org.

LEXINGTON

Lexington's Other Attractions

The horse may be the symbol of the Kentucky Bluegrass, but it is far from the only attraction the area has to offer. There are also history and heritage, culture and cuisine, museums and music, natural beauty and man-made monuments. The Bluegrass region offers something for everyone.

Historic Homes

In the early part of the 19th century, when most of the country west of the Allegheny Mountains was still frontier, Lexington was a thriving community, home to sophisticated, cultured citizens, many of them prominent in politics, horse racing, business, and the arts. Lexington's citizenry was so erudite and educated that the city was referred to as "the Athens of the West."

During the half-century between 1800 and 1850, Lexington's population read like a "Who's Who of American History" — John Wesley Hunt, Kentucky's first millionaire, and his grandson, Confederate general John Hunt Morgan; Mary Todd Lincoln, Joseph Bryan, plantation owner and great-nephew of Daniel Boone; and towering over them all — Henry Clay, the "Great Compromiser." As testament to Lexington's love affair with its past, their homes have been preserved as museums.

ASHLAND, THE HENRY CLAY ESTATE

Henry Clay, who was much admired by Lincoln for his states-manship, built his beloved estate, Ashland, in the same year that Mary Todd Lincoln's childhood home was completed, and lived there with his family until 1852. During that time the 18-room Italianate-style mansion saw many of history's greats pass through its doors, including Daniel Webster; Jefferson Davis, a classmate of Clay's at Transylvania College; William Henry Harrison, who was president-elect at the time; and the Marquis de Lafayette.

One of America's greatest statesmen, Clay served as congressman, senator, Speaker of the House, Secretary of State, and three-time presidential candidate. He forged his destiny in the nation's capital during the time of its greatest unrest, in the years leading up to the Civil War. That chaos made returning to his 672-acre estate, lined with willowy sycamore trees, where he raised corn, hemp, tobacco, and cattle, all the more pleasurable, and he considered Ashland a haven, a place of refuge from the harsh political realities of the day. He persuaded his friend Benjamin Latrobe, architect of the U.S. Capitol, to design a portion of the estate — the two wings on either side of the original house. The finest feature of the house is generally considered to be the circular rotunda over the octagonal library.

Today's visitors will enjoy the same sense of tranquility that Clay did as they tour the house and stroll the beautiful grounds (20 acres of the original 672 remain), complete with a formal English parterre garden. Also on the grounds is the Gingko Tree Café, located in the former carriage house and the perfect place for a light lunch.

◇◇◇◇◇◇◇◇◇◇◇◇◇◇◇◇

120 Sycamore Rd. (859) 266-8581. www.henryclay.org.
Monday–Saturday, 10:00 a.m.–4:00 p.m.; Sunday, 1:00–4:00 p.m.
Admission: adults, $7; children, $4; students, $3; under 6, free.

HOPEMONT

John Wesley Hunt, Kentucky's first millionaire and a business associate of John Jacob Astor, chose the peaceful oasis of Gratz Park for his mansion, Hopemont. But it was his grandson who gave the house its cachet. John Hunt Morgan, dubbed the "Thunderbolt of the Confederacy" by adoring Southerners and the "King of Horse Thieves" by Northern sympathizers, was a figure of epic proportions. Among the many legends attached to him is the one that claims he rode his mare Black Bess through the front door of the house, leaned from the saddle to kiss his mother, and made his escape out the back door, Yankees in hot pursuit.

Whether that actually happened depends on one's capacity for romance. However, it is fact that Morgan planned many of his guerilla raids while hiding out in the house. Hopemont must surely have been the scene of much excitement during the Civil War, as the house across the park, the Bodley-Bullock Mansion (also open for tours by appointment only, 859-259-1266), briefly served as the headquarters for the Union Army.

The third famous scion of the family to live in the house was Dr. Thomas Hunt Morgan, the first Kentuckian to win a Nobel Prize.

Hopemont, completed in 1814 and saved from demolition in 1955 by the Blue Grass Trust for Historic Preservation, is a showcase museum, best known architecturally for the beautiful fan-shaped chancel over the front door and spiral staircase in the front hall, and historically for its extensive collection of Civil War memorabilia.

201 North Mill St. (859) 233-3290. www.bluegrasstrust.org/hunt-morgan.html. Wednesday–Friday and on Sunday, 1:00–4:00 p.m.; Saturday, 10:00 a.m.–3:00 p.m. Admission: adults, $7; seniors, $6; students and children, $4.

MARY TODD LINCOLN HOUSE

At first glance, the modest two-story brick building on West Main Street seems an unlikely choice to become the first house museum in America to honor a First Lady. Yet, in 1977, the girlhood home of Mary Todd Lincoln, wife of the nation's 16th president, was brought to the attention of the American public.

Completed in 1806, the 14-room Georgian-style house was home to the Todd family from 1832 to 1849, and many historians believe that Mary, dogged by tragedy throughout much of her life, spent her happiest years here, from age 13 to 21. After her marriage to fellow Kentuckian Abraham Lincoln, Mary brought her husband to visit her childhood home, where he supposedly spent hours ensconced in the library, making the acquaintance of his "beau ideal" of a statesman, Henry Clay. On a less enlightened note, it was also here that he witnessed slavery, both in the Todd household and at the slave market on nearby Cheapside. Today the house contains period furniture, portraits, and furnishings from both the Todd and Lincoln families, as well as memorabilia ranging from a chocolate pot Mary purchased at Tiffany's to the original Ford's Theater playbill from the evening of Lincoln's assassination.

578 West Main St. www.mtlhouse.org.
Monday–Saturday, 10:00 a.m.–4:00 p.m. Admission: adults, $7; children, 6-12, $4; under 6, free.

WAVELAND STATE HISTORIC SITE

Now the Kentucky Life Museum, the 10-room Waveland mansion was built in 1847 by Joseph Bryan, a great-nephew of Daniel Boone. Among the finest examples of Greek Revival architecture in the state, its features include a portico with Ionic columns and the main doorway topped by a frieze that is a copy of the north entrance to the Erechtheum on the Acropolis in Athens, Greece. The grand symmetrical style of the house was extremely popular in Kentucky in the years leading up to the Civil War.

Waveland, in fact, exemplified plantation life, with its acres devoted to grain and hemp and its stable of blooded Standardbred horses.

The mansion sits atop a knoll surrounded by 15 acres of farmland that include an herb garden, flower garden, and orchard, as well as many meticulously restored outbuildings: slave quarters, fireplace kitchen, ice house, smoke house, and blacksmith shop.

225 Waveland Museum La., south of downtown, off Nicholasville Road (U.S. 27). (859) 272-3611. www.kystateparks.com. Monday–Saturday, 9:00 a.m.–5:00 p.m.; and Sunday, 1:00–5:00 p.m. Admission: adults, $7; seniors, $6; students, $4.

FYI: Visitors can see all four houses with a combination ticket that costs $15, good for one year from date of purchase. This ticket must be purchased from the Lexington Convention & Visitors Bureau. (859) 233-1221.

Museums

EXPLORIUM OF LEXINGTON

This interactive art and science museum is a family favorite. Permanent exhibits include Brainzilla, an exploration of the human brain; Hold Your Horses, which gives a child's perspective on Kentucky's favorite animal; Wonder Woods, a nature area designed especially for toddlers, and The Bubble Zone, where it is difficult to tell who is having more fun — children or their parents.

**440 W. Short St. (859) 258-3253. www.explorium.com.
Tuesday–Saturday, 10:00 a.m.–5:00 p.m.;
Sunday, 1:00–5:00 p.m. Admission: $6.**

HEADLEY-WHITNEY MUSEUM

George Headley may have been an accomplished artist (studying at L'Ecole des Beaux Arts in Paris) but he was also a crackerjack marketer. During the late 1930s and '40s, when he operated an exclusive jewelry boutique at the Bel-Air Hotel in Los Angeles, he would often entice potential customers sunning poolside by sending his dachshund Ernie out to model a diamond or emerald necklace. A bejeweled Ernie was an effective marketing tool as Headley, during his tenure in Tinseltown, numbered among his clients Mae West, Judy Garland, Joan Crawford, and a bevy of socialites, jet-setters, and international royalty.

Thus, it was only natural when Headley moved to Lexington in the early 1950s to take over the family farm, La Belle, he would seek an outlet for his artistic nature. He found it in designing one-of-a-kind bibelots, created from precious and semi-precious stones. Today, visitors to the Headley-Whitney Museum, picturesquely situated among Thoroughbred horse farms on Old Frankfort Pike, can marvel at the fruits of his labor. The museum complex, an affiliate of the Smithsonian, consists of four distinctive areas — the jewel room, library, shell grotto, and main museum.

Inside the tiny jewel room — designed to look like a jewelry box with its dark interior and low ambient lighting — are some of his most beautiful pieces. There is a pair of turtles with gold underbellies, shell bodies, limbs, tails, and heads of pale pink and orange coral, and diamond eyes. A terra cotta pigeon has ruby eyes and feet of pink gold and sports a gold pendant with rubies and diamonds. A mask of Bacchus, Roman god of wine, is fashioned of delicate coral and backed with a tangle of gold grapevines. Another bibelot, the Bird Cage, features the figure of a Chinese woman intricately carved of Persian turquoise and sitting on a cushion of lapis lazuli inside a gold cage accented with diamonds and sapphires.

The library reflects a number of Headley's favorite architectural motifs, including a sloped Thai roof and Greek columns. The room's eclectic collection of objects features a pair of candlesticks made in London from ostrich eggs and ivory and an Indian elephant tusk from the late 18th century carved in a lacy pattern.

Headley converted a three-car garage into the shell grotto, a fantasy pavilion modeled after architectural "follies" of 17th and 18th century France, England, and Italy. He worked for nearly a year gluing thousands of shells and polished stones to walls, doors, and window moldings. From the coral slabs of the floor to the mosaics on the ceiling, he created an exotic sea environment. The grotto contains twin heads of Aphrodite and Neptune sculpted in seashells and coral, an ornate birdcage fashioned from seashells, and an iron chandelier encrusted with scallops, cowries, and nautilus shells.

The decorative arts museum occupies the complex's main building. Housing a permanent collection of porcelain and silver as well as the dollhouse collection of horse farm owner Marylou Whitney (the houses are exact replicas of her Lexington mansion), it also hosts a wide range of traveling exhibitions.

4435 Old Frankfort Pike. (859) 255-6653.
www.headley-whitney.org. Tuesday–Friday,
10:00 a.m.–5:00 p.m.; Saturday and Sunday, noon–5:00 p.m.
Admission to the museum and the Marylou Whitney Gardens:
Adults, $10; students and seniors, $7; under 5, free.

LEXINGTON HISTORY MUSEUM

Lexington's old courthouse has been transformed into a museum showcasing local and regional history. Among the permanent exhibitions are "Athens of the West," a look at Lexington's role as a cultural center in the commonwealth; "In Black and White," which depicts African-American life in the Bluegrass from the Civil War through Civil Rights; and the "Keeneland Legacy," showcasing the importance of Keeneland Race Course to the community and the region. The museum is Lexington's only free historic site.

215 West Main St. (859) 254-0530.
www.lexingtonhistorymuseum.org.
Monday–Friday, noon–4:00 p.m.; Saturday, 10:00 a.m.–4:00 p.m.

UNIVERSITY OF KENTUCKY ART MUSEUM

Located in the Singletary Center for the Arts on the University of Kentucky campus, the museum has a permanent collection

DID YOU KNOW

In the 1930s, the Lexington *Herald* had a standing offer to give free papers on any day that a horse bred within a 50-mile radius of Lexington failed to win a race at any major track.

of some 3,800 works by American and European artists, including paintings, sculptures, prints and drawings, photographs, and decorative arts. Fewer in number, but of equal quality, are the museum's collections of African, Asian, and Latin American art.

Among the permanent pieces in the collection are works by Mary Cassatt, Gilbert Stuart, James McNeill Whistler, Jasper Johns, and Andy Warhol. In addition to the permanent exhibits, temporary exhibitions range from the art of ancient Egypt to the abstract works of Robert Motherwell.

Rose Street & Euclid Avenue. (859) 257-5716. www.uky.edu/ArtMuseum. Tuesday, Wednesday, Thursday, Saturday, and Sunday, noon–5:00 p.m.; Friday, noon–8:00 p.m. Free admission to permanent collections.

Nature Preserves

THE ARBORETUM

A joint project of the University of Kentucky and the Lexington/Fayette Urban County Government, the Arboretum is the State Botanical Garden of Kentucky. Its 100 acres offer year-round color in a number of distinctive gardens: Rose, Fragrance, Perennial, Annual, Herb, and Rock. Another feature, the Arboretum Woods, is an ecological restoration, while the Walk Across Kentucky is a two-mile paved walkway with markers identifying the native flora of Kentucky's seven physiographic regions: Bluegrass, Knobs, Pennyrile, Appalachian Plateau, Cumberland, Shawnee Hills, and Mississippi Embayment.

500 Alumni Dr., across from Commonwealth Stadium on the UK campus. www.ca.uky.edu/arboretum. Open 365 days a year with free admission. (859) 257-6955.

MCCONNELL SPRINGS

Considered the site where Lexington was founded (see Chapter 1), McConnell Springs is a 26-acre serene oasis on the outskirts of downtown, more suited to phosphorescent blue indigo buntings and jackrabbits than the humans who live and work close by. Hikers on McConnell Springs' two miles of trails will see a floral carpet composed of some 130 species, including great blue lobelia, yellow beggar's tick, scarlet cardinal's flower, pink swamp milkweed, blue flag iris, lavender appendaged waterleaf, and multicolored jewelweed.

Hikers may also encounter any of the numerous species of urban wildlife that call the springs home — garter snakes, box turtles, groundhogs, sharp-shinned hawks, even a shy red fox — somewhat surprising as the springs are within earshot of New Circle Road, one of the busiest throughways in the city.

In addition to nature lovers, archaeology buffs will find the springs fascinating. Already unearthed are rock fences dating back to the 1800s and ruins that indicate the presence of an early 19th-century grist mill, both of which can be seen from the hiking trails. Archaeologists continue to uncover trace evidence of early life at McConnell Springs, which in the years after its discovery served as a gunpowder factory, the water supply for a distillery, and a horse and dairy farm.

But it's the springs' natural beauty that draws visitors to such areas as the Blue Hole, the first of two major springs, and the Boils, the second spring. The Blue Hole has been a source of mystery since its earliest discovery by Indian tribes who marveled at the electric blue of the water. Its color comes from the way the sun strikes the pool through the dense canopy of trees, as well as from the depth of the water, estimated at 15 feet.

Water from the Blue Hole flows underground through limestone bedrock to emerge at the second spring. Known as the Boils because of the way the water bubbles on the surface, the spring disappears here as well, emerging at the cave-like formation of the Final Sink. Here, the waters flow underground again until they re-emerge a third of a mile away at Preston's Cave and join the Wolf Run Creek to flow into the Town Branch of Elkhorn Creek, Lexington's major body of water.

The area around the Blue Hole has become a prime example of a forest wetland environment, where a variety of native wildflowers, rushes, and grasses help hold soil in place, thus restoring and preserving the biological richness of McConnell Springs.

McConnell Springs is inside New Circle Road just off Old Frankfort Pike a few miles from downtown Lexington. www.McConnellSprings.org. It is open free of charge daily from 9:00 a.m.–5:00 p.m. (859) 225-4073.

RAVEN RUN NATURE SANCTUARY

A 734-acre nature preserve that falls within the Lexington city limits, Raven Run backs up to the palisades of the Kentucky River, making it the embodiment of a pristine wilderness, home to wildlife (including deer), 200 species of birds, and 600 species of plants, including 56 varieties of trees. It is particularly beautiful in the spring and early summer when wildflowers blanket the ground.

Raven Run offers 10 miles of hiking trails for every level of hiker which cover meadow, forest, and streambed ecosystems. The Freedom Trail and the Green Trails are the easiest, with the Yellow Trail (also called the Flower Bowl Trail) the most difficult;

an extension of this trail, Pioneer Road leading to the Kentucky River, is extremely steep. Blue Trails connect one trail to another and White Trails take hikers to points of interest such as an old grist mill on the creek bank. The four-mile Red Trail is the main trail loop and is moderately difficult; it is the most popular of the trails as it takes hikers to the Overlook, a scenic vista above the river palisades.

⊗⊗⊗⊗⊗⊗⊗⊗⊗

588 Jack's Creek Pike. Take Old Richmond Road to Jack's Creek Pike. Follow Jack's Creek for several miles and the entrance to Raven Run will be on the left. Open daily (except for major holidays) from 9:00 a.m.–5:00 p.m. All visitors must register at the Nature Center and are required to be out of the sanctuary by closing time. No alcohol, pets, or camping allowed. (859) 272-6105.

Wineries

Most everyone knows that Kentucky is the home of bourbon, America's only native spirit, but very few know that the state was also the site of the country's first commercial vineyard, planted by the winemaker to the Marquis de Lafayette in the 18th century. While there is no formal wine trail as there is a Bourbon Trail, visitors can find several wineries in Lexington and its environs.

CHRISMAN MILL VINEYARDS

Driving up the winding hill to Chrisman Mill's tasting room, you can't help but sense a little bit of Tuscany in the Bluegrass, and that feeling is only enhanced when you get a whiff of the homemade wine breads made daily in the winery's kitchen.

Chrisman Mill is known for its bronze and silver medal-winning cabernets — sauvignon and franc, as well as its vidal blancs, the latter offered both alone and combined with Chancellor in a Sweet Jasmine Rose blend. Tours and tastings (five wines for $3) are available, and you can also enjoy an al fresco picnic surrounded by lush grape vines. Or, if you want something a bit more formal, Chrisman Mill offers twice-monthly Friday Night Tuscan Dinners in the rustic restaurant (reservations essential, check the Web site for dates).

2385 Chrisman Mill Rd., Nicholasville. (859) 881-5007. www.chrismanmill.com. Monday–Saturday, 11:00 a.m.–8:00 p.m.; Sunday, noon–6:00 p.m.

EQUUS RUN VINEYARDS

From Lexington, it's a short 20-minute drive to Midway where, nestled amidst picturesque stone fences and rolling fields you'll find one of Kentucky's most celebrated wineries. The loamy soil and limestone-enhanced water of the central Kentucky Bluegrass have allowed Equus Run to be a boutique winery that produces mega-wines. Its excellent offerings include a wide range of varietals: chardonnay, blush, vidal blanc, merlot, cabernet sauvignon, and Riesling, many of which have won awards in international competitions.

Equus Run offers one complimentary guided tour a day beginning at 1:30 p.m. Highlights of the 30-minute tour are the renovated tobacco barn now used for the production of the wine, the exquisite flower gardens, and the vineyards themselves. If you wish, you can explore at a more leisurely pace on a self-guided walking tour. Equus Run's tastings are a real bargain — six wines for $2 and you get to take home your souvenir wine glass.

1280 Moores Mill Rd., Midway. (859) 846-9463.
www.equusrunvineyards.com. April–October,
Monday–Saturday, 11:00 a.m.–7:00 p.m.; November–March,
Monday–Saturday, 11:00 a.m.–5:00 p.m. Check the winery's
Web site for dates of the popular "Concerts in the Vineyard" series.

JEAN FARRIS WINERY & BISTRO

This family-owned winery manages to be both upscale (the wine room and bistro are the ultimate in retro-chic) and homey (summer evenings on the patio are a favorite with locals and visitors) at the same time. The food is French country-inspired cuisine (they offer dinner Tuesday through Saturday and Saturday and Sunday brunch) and their wines have taken bronze, silver, and gold medals at national and international competitions. Tastings offer several wine flights to choose from, ranging from $4 to $11.

6825 Old Richmond Rd. (859) 263-9463. www.jeanfarris.com.
Tuesday–Sunday, noon–9:00 p.m.; Saturday,
10:30 a.m.–9:30 p.m.

TALON WINERY & VINEYARDS

Lexington's answer to the romance of Napa and Sonoma, Talon is located on what was once prime horse pastures. Its 300 acres of sharply rolling farmland are dotted with ponds and punctuated by red-roofed barns. Complimentary tours offer a sneak peek at the vineyards, processing center, and traditional Kentucky oak barrels.

Tastings, priced at $3 for three wines or $5 for six wines, showcase not only chardonnay, Traminette, cabernet sauvignon, and specialty blends Bluegrass Blush and Moondance, but the ambiance of the tasting room — the 18th-century farmhouse at historic Fair View Farm, or, in nice weather, the deck overlooking the vineyards. Guests can also choose a spot for a picnic on the grounds, and if you want something besides hot dogs and potato chips, the winery gift shop offers a variety of exotic foods that will make any picnic a feast.

7086 Tates Creek Rd. (859) 971-3214. www.talonwine.com. Monday–Thursday, 10:00 a.m.–6:00 p.m.; Friday and Saturday, 10:00 a.m.–7:00 p.m.

Music

WOODSONGS OLD TIME RADIO HOUR

The meandering journey from upstate New York to the border town of Laredo, Texas, to the mountains of Appalachia in Mousie, Kentucky, may seem like an odd career arc, but it has paid off handsomely for Michael Jonathan. The folk singer/songwriter/concert performer and self-proclaimed "tree-hugger" commands a worldwide radio and television audience who tune in every Monday night to his broadcast of Woodsongs Old Time Radio Hour, recorded live from Lexington's historic Kentucky Theater. They're listening in Chenega Bay, Alaska; and Hawkes Bay, New Zealand; in Boise and Boston; in Serbia and Slovenia; in Queanbeyan, New South Wales, Australia; and in Bergen Op Zoom, Holland.

Just what are they listening to?

Bluegrass and blues, folk and country, rhythm & blues, and Rock-a-billy, and chances are they have never heard of many of the artists. For Woodsongs is radio's only syndicated live-audience program dedicated to artists who are talented and innovative, but not exactly rocking the Grammys or showing up regularly on VH1 or MTV.

Still, Woodsongs does attract its share of stars, from the late folk legend Odetta to Dust Bowl troubadour and poet Ramblin' Jack Elliott, friend of Woody Guthrie, mentor to Bob Dylan, and inspiration to Mick Jagger. Other Monday performances might find the likes of bluegrass diva Rhonda Vincent, country favorites Lee Roy Parnell and Rodney Crowell, gospel group Blind Boys of Alabama, and Celtic Band Gaelic Storm in the lineup.

The format for Woodsongs Old Time Radio Hour reflects the personality of its creator and host — "Woody Guthrie in a cyber world," as he's been described, or a hipper version of Garrison Keillor. Decked out in jeans and a black leather jacket, Jonathan presides over Lake Woebegon's just-as-quirky Southern counterpart.

In a setting reminiscent of the early days of Nashville's Grand Old Opry when a heart-rending ballad of love gone wrong was followed by a commercial for Martha White's self-rising flour, Jonathan interacts with the audiences — many of whom are regulars — that pack the Kentucky Theater every Monday night. And while his marketing savvy has taken Woodsongs to podcasts, webcasts, and most recently, to PBS stations across the country, it is the cozy feel of sittin' on the front porch strummin' the banjo

DID YOU KNOW

Actor Edwin Booth, brother of
Abraham Lincoln's assassin, John Wilkes Booth,
performed the role of Shakespeare's
Richard III at Lexington's
Opera House.

that defines the program and keeps bringing in the crowds.

Woodsongs Old Time Radio Hour is produced live every Monday night at the Kentucky Theatre at 214 East Main St. www.woodsongs.com. For show schedules and reservations, call (859) 252-8888.

Other Attractions Worth Checking Out

GRATZ PARK HISTORIC DISTRICT

Tucked between downtown and the campus of Transylvania College is one of Lexington's most charming neighborhoods, now listed on the National Register of Historic Places. With its colorful Federal-style row houses, it is a more genteel version of Charleston's Catfish Row.

In 1781 Transylvania Seminary established its campus on the acreage. A devastating fire that destroyed the main building forced the campus to move across the street; all that remains is the old kitchen in the northeast quadrant of the park.

Following the college's move, Gratz Park became a residential neighborhood, with a host of colorful characters in residence over the years: Benjamin Gratz, an early Lexington businessman for whom the park is named; General Thomas Bodley, a veteran of the War of 1812; Confederate General John Hunt Morgan, and Mrs. William Cassius Goodloe, the widow of a former U.S. Ambassador to Belgium. It is still home to some of Lexington's most distinguished citizens.

A lovely Fountain of Youth honors Lexingtonian James Lane Allen, a 19th-century writer described as "Kentucky's first important novelist." A block from the park is the former law office of Henry Clay, as well as the charming Gratz Park Inn (see Chapter 11).

RUPP ARENA

The University of Kentucky boasts the winningest college basketball program in NCAA history, and this arena in downtown Lexington is the playground of the seven-time national champion Wildcats. During the season, a seat in the 23,000-seat arena is the hottest ticket in town, and if you are lucky enough to score one, you might find yourself sitting next to the Cats' No. 1 fan, actress and former UK student Ashley Judd, who attends many of the home games.

After basketball season, Rupp Arena attracts major concerts and events.

Downtown next to the Hyatt Regency Hotel and the Lexington Convention Center. www.rupparena.com.

VICTORIAN SQUARE

This colorful collection of Victorian-style buildings across from Triangle Park has been at the core of Lexington's downtown area since the 1880s, first housing saloons, boarding houses, and business establishments, and following a 1985 renovation, shops, restaurants, and bars all facing a central covered atrium. Shoppers can find boutiques specializing in men's and women's clothing, jewelry, and arts and crafts; diners can select from restaurants such as the Brazilian-themed De Vassa Bar & Café and the local favorite, deSha's; and nightlife options range from pubs to a piano bar. The Artists' Attic on the fourth floor allows visitors to watch artists at work.

Corner of West Main Street and North Broadway. www.victoriansquareshoppes.com.

DID YOU KNOW

Belle Brezing, a notorious madam in Lexington, was supposedly the inspiration for Belle Watling, the notorious madam in Margaret Mitchell's novel *Gone With the Wind*.

LATROBE'S POPE VILLA

This Lexington mansion is one of only three remaining buildings in the country designed by Benjamin Latrobe, one of the architects of the U.S. Capitol building. Commissioned by Senator John Pope and his wife Eliza, it was built between 1810 and 1811. Influenced by Italian architect Andrea Palladio, Latrobe designed the villa as a perfect square with a domed circular rotunda. It is being carefully restored by the Blue Grass Trust for Historic Preservation and is not open for tours.

326 Grosvenor Ave. (859) 253-0362. www.popevilla.org.

LEXINGTON CEMETERY

Considered one of America's most beautiful cemeteries, it is listed as a national arboretum and listed in the National Register of Historic Places for landscape design. Opened in 1849, the 170-acre cemetery is the burial place for distinguished Lexingtonians ranging from Henry Clay (his monument can be seen towering above the trees) and John Hunt Morgan to legendary Kentucky basketball coach Adolph Rupp. There are 200 species of trees on the grounds, which are especially beautiful in spring when the dogwood, redbud, magnolia, pink weeping cherry, and Bradford pear trees are blossoming.

833 West Main St. (859) 255-5522. www.lexcem.org.

LEXINGTON LEGENDS

The Legends are the Class A minor league affiliate of the Houston Astros baseball team and play in the South Atlantic League. Beginning in April, they play 70 regular season home games at Applebee Park north of downtown Lexington.

207 Legends La., off of North Broadway. (859) 252-4487. www.lexingtonlegends.com.

LEXINGTON OPERA HOUSE

One of downtown Lexington's historic gems, the opera house was built in 1886 and during its heyday played host to every important entertainer of the day. Just a few of the stars who graced its stage were Sarah Bernhardt, Ethel Barrymore, Al Jolson, Fanny Brice, W.C. Fields, Will Rogers, and Harry Houdini. Their time here is chronicled in the celebrity portrait gallery on the first balcony level.

The last live performance was in 1926, after which the Opera House deteriorated. In the early 1970s the building was slated for demolition when local philanthropists rescued it and restored it (another renovation took place in 2008). Today's audiences will see the red velvet curtains, grand staircase, ornate opera boxes, Chippendale-style mirrors, and French crystal chandeliers that once made it the grandest theater in the commonwealth.

The Opera House is home to the Lexington Ballet Company, Kentucky Ballet Theater, Lexington Children's Theater, and the University of Kentucky Opera Theatre, as well as a full season of national Broadway touring productions.

401 W. Short St. (859) 233-4567. www.lexingtonoperahouse.com.

7

Louisville's
Other Attractions

The "River City" is Kentucky's largest metropolis and, as such, home to a wealth of attractions no visitor to the commonwealth should miss. Best known as the site of Churchill Downs and the Kentucky Derby, the city is also a starting point of the Bourbon Trail and the location of a Tony Award-winning theater, an acclaimed art museum, and a nationally recognized zoo. In Louisville you can follow the exploits of the "boys of summer" at a unique baseball museum, pay tribute to "the greatest" at the Muhammad Ali Center, or take a trip back in time aboard the *Belle of Louisville* paddlewheeler as it plies the waters of the Ohio River. Louisville has something for everyone, but first, you have to learn to pronounce the city's name correctly. Despite how sportscasters — who should know better — pronounce it, it is not "Louie-ville." Neither is it "Lewis-ville." The correct pronunciation is "Loo-uh-vul." Now that's not so hard, is it?

Museums

SPEED ART MUSEUM

A reclining bronze by English sculptor Henry Moore at first appears a curious juxtaposition against two sepia-toned "before and after" photographs of Native Americans — one in traditional garb and the other after they had been "Anglicized" — but anyone familiar with the Speed Museum would not be surprised by the eclectic nature of the art on display.

The museum, Kentucky's largest, and often referred to as one of the great art repositories of the mid-South, has more than 13,000 works spanning some 6,000 years of history. There's Picasso, of course, but there's also Swiss painter Paul Klee. Henri Matisse, a French Fauvist painter, shares space with Helen Frankenthaler, an American abstract expressionist. Both the Impressionist paintings of Mary Cassatt and the Art Deco sculpture of Paul Manship have found a home at the Speed.

The ancient Greeks, Romans, Etruscans, and Egyptians are represented, as are West African tribes such as the Yoruba and Dan, and the Indian tribes of the Great Plains — the Sioux, Cheyenne, Crow, Arapaho, and Kiowa.

The museum opened in 1927 as the J.B. Speed Memorial Museum, created by Hattie Bishop Speed as a tribute to her husband, businessman and philanthropist James Breckenridge Speed. From the beginning, it proved a huge success with Kentucky art lovers who, lacking a topnotch museum of their own, had felt somewhat intimidated by their cultured brethren east of the Alleghenies.

Over the years the Speed has amassed an impressive collection of European painting and sculpture, particularly 17th-century Dutch and Flemish and 18th-century French paintings and Baroque tapestries, but there are other notable works as well, including paintings by Italian Renaissance artists Fra Bartolomeo and Giambattista Tiepolo, and French Impressionist Claude Monet and Realist Gustave Courbet.

The Speed has also nurtured homegrown artists. Its Kentucky collection showcases painting, sculpture, and decorative arts created by and for Kentuckians, primarily during the 1800s when much of the state was still frontier. The works give a sense of the range and quality of artistic achievement, and of the evolution of styles and tastes during this important time in Kentucky's history.

The Speed — like the art and artists it showcases — remains fluid, exhibiting not only such recognized masterpieces as Rembrandt's *Portrait of a Woman* and Monet's *Church at Varengeville*, but more modern acquisitions such as Andy Warhol's *Birmingham Race Riots* and Winslow Homer's *The Ratcatcher's Daughter*.

◇◦◦◇◦◦◇◦◇◦◦◇◦◦◇◦

**2035 South Third St. (502) 634-2700. www.speedmuseum.org.
Tuesday, Wednesday, and Friday, 10:30 a.m.–4:00 p.m.;
Thursday, 10:30 a.m.–8:00 p.m.; Saturday, 10:30 a.m.–5:00 p.m.;
Sunday, noon–5:00 p.m. Free admission,
except for special exhibitions.**

LOUISVILLE SLUGGER MUSEUM

Mel Allen's rich, deep voice bellows over the airwaves, "Mantle swings. He hits a long fly deep into right field. It's up; it's up; it's OUTTA THERE!"

You've time-traveled back to the 1950s when Allen was the voice of the New York Yankees and the Mick was routinely hitting balls "outta there." Allen is just one of the colorful baseball announcers whose broadcasts can be heard at the Louisville Slugger Museum by simply pushing a button. Push another button and you can hear the smooth-as-silk voice of Harry Caray, synonymous with the Chicago Cubs. Another push and you hear Detroit Tiger announcer Ernie Harwell describing America's national pastime as a "ballet without music; a drama without words."

The Slugger Museum, which opened in 1996 on Main Street,

may be just one of an ever-expanding number of attractions on the city's Museum Row, but to hardcore baseball fans it's the Hermitage of home runs, the Louvre of line drives, the Smithsonian of swings. The five-story-tall baseball bat — the world's largest — casually propped against the building lets you know you have arrived at the literal birthplace of the Major League bat.

In 1884, John "Bud" Hillerich, son of a German immigrant woodworker, made baseball history when he crafted a wooden bat for Pete "the Gladiator" Browning, a player for the Louisville Eclipse baseball team of the American Association. It was the first Louisville Slugger ever made, and over the next century, some 8,000 professional baseball players, including 80 percent of Hall of Fame hitters, have exclusively used bats made by the Hillerich and Bradsby Company.

The Slugger Museum is a shrine to the players, the bats, and the magic they made together. Visitors can see that first Slugger bat used by Browning in 1884 and the one used 50 years later by Babe Ruth, on September 29, 1934, the day that he hit his last home run as a New York Yankee. They can see bats swung by Ty Cobb, Lou Gehrig, Jackie Robinson, Roberto Clemente, Joe DiMaggio, Hank Aaron, and Ted Williams.

A good introduction to the 14,000-square-foot museum is the short film, *The Heart of the Game*, which will put you in the mood for hot dogs, beer, and "batter up." Following the film, walk through

DID YOU KNOW

Louisville has given the world the song *Happy Birthday*, composed by two Louisville kindergarten teachers, sisters Patty and Mildred Hill, and chewing gum (invented by Louisvillian John Colgan in 1873; unfortunately, he never got around to patenting it).

a replica of a locker room into a full-sized dugout, and step onto the museum's playing field. You can almost hear the roar of the crowd as you tap your toe against home plate. Next, stroll through the museum's galleries with rare collections of photos, equipment, artifacts, interactive displays, and special traveling exhibits.

But for a sheer adrenaline boost, nothing equals standing behind the replica of home plate and, without flinching, watching as a virtual fast ball comes straight at you, delivered by the Red Sox's Pedro Martinez or the Astros' Roger Clemens. It seems an apt moment to recall one of Babe Ruth, the Sultan of Swat's, most famous quotes, "I swing big, with everything I've got."

You can also tour the assembly line where the bats are still turned out at the factory next door.

◇ ◇◇◇◇◇ ◇◇ ◇◇◇◇◇ ◇◇

800 West Main St. (502) 588-7228 or (877) 775-8443. www.sluggermuseum.com. Monday–Saturday, 9:00 a.m.–5:00 p.m.; Sunday, noon–5:00 p.m. Admission: adults, $10; seniors, $9; children 6-12, $5; 5 and under, free.

MUHAMMAD ALI CENTER

He "floated like a butterfly and stung like a bee" all the way to the World Heavyweight title on three separate occasions. He was stripped of his title after a conscience-driven and controversial refusal to serve in the U.S. military during the Vietnam War. He was lauded for his humanitarian efforts and reviled for his conversion to Islam from Christianity, and for changing his name to Muhammad Ali from Cassius Clay. He has been called the greatest athlete of the 20th century.

But we know him best by the nickname he gave himself as a brash 20-something out to conquer the boxing world — the Greatest.

His odyssey from then-segregated Louisville to a gold medal at the 1960 Rome Olympics to the pinnacle of the boxing world has been a long one; his transformation from Cassius Clay — who might have gone down the troubled road of other black youth of his time — to Muhammad Ali — who has walked with presidents and kings — has often been a difficult one.

Encompassing two-and-a-half floors of exhibition space, the Muhammad Ali Center takes visitors on this odyssey and through this transformation. This is no typical sports museum; it is equal parts elegance (the prominent atrium display of his Presidential Medal of Freedom) and kitsch (the equally prominent display of his bejeweled robe, a gift from Elvis Presley before a fight in Las Vegas). It is pluck — videos of his youthful boasting of how pretty he was — and pathos — videos of his Parkinsons-wracked body painstakingly lighting the torch at the 1996 Olympic Games in Atlanta. It is crass consumerism — his 1977 Rolls Royce Corniche — and the best of the human spirit — a collage by children from 141 countries in which they express their hopes and dreams. This is not a place that lionizes a sports figure as much as a place that focuses on the man himself.

While boxing aficionados will have plenty to keep them occupied — a dynamic multimedia presentation of Ali's victories in the ring as well as his jocular jousting with sportscaster Howard Cosell — those who don't know a KO from a K-9 will find plenty to keep them entertained, amused, and often, on edge. The entertainment and amusement can be found in his clever cartoons and drawings and his poetic ramblings that were a precursor to modern day rap. The edginess stems from tableaus such as the 1950s Jim Crow lunch counter and the violent upheavals of the 1960s Civil Rights movement where newsreels juxtapose film clips of Malcolm X with those of George Wallace.

The museum has some 40 interactive exhibits in 19 languages, which are divided into pavilions depicting the six core values that Ali lived by: respect, confidence, conviction, dedication, spirituality, and giving. Some of these exhibits show him welcoming Nelson Mandela upon his release from prison, delivering food and medical supplies to the needy in Third World countries, and ladling soup in kitchens across America.

Like the man it honors, the museum at times floats like a butterfly and at others, stings like a bee.

◇·◇◇·◇◇·◇◇·◇◇·◇

144 N. Sixth St. (502) 584-9254. www.alicenter.org.
Tuesday–Saturday, 9:30 a.m.–5:00 p.m.; Sunday, noon–5:00 p.m.
Admission ranges from $4 for children to $9 for adults.

KENTUCKY MUSEUM OF ART AND CRAFT

Located in a renovated building in the city's historic West Main Street corridor, the museum offers four floors dedicated to the commonwealth's justly famous arts and crafts tradition. A curved staircase leads visitors to three galleries showcasing arts and crafts both traditional — handmade quilts and handcrafted furniture — and modern — delicately blown glass objects and intricately designed jewelry.

From innovative woodwork to creative textiles, the Kentucky Museum of Art and Craft has it all. Much of what you see can be purchased, but there is a permanent collection in the third-floor Brown-Forman Gallery. While prices reflect the quality of work (meaning it's not cheap), it is a remarkably un-stodgy place to browse (visitors are actually encouraged to touch the art). When you are finished checking out the exhibits, save time to wander through the first floor gift shop where some 200 different artists have their wares for sale.

715 West Main St. (502) 589-0102. www.kentuckyarts.org.
Monday–Friday, 10:00 a.m.–5:00 p.m.;
Saturday, 11:00 a.m.–5:00 p.m. Admission: adults, $5;
seniors, $4; under 12, free.

FRAZIER INTERNATIONAL HISTORY MUSEUM

A museum must be special if it is chosen by Great Britain's Royal Armouries to be the only museum outside the United Kingdom to showcase some of its military treasures, and the Frazier doesn't disappoint.

Even if you consider yourself a pacifist and the mere thought of spending a couple of hours looking at weapons of war gives you the shivers, you will find the museum pleasantly surprising. The Frazier's exhibits are only partly dedicated to weaponry, ranging from longbows used by the English archers at the Battle of Anjou to Colt .45's used by every lawman and desperado in the American West to Teddy Roosevelt's African safari hunting rifle.

The rest of the museum provides an opportunity for visitors to embark on a 1,000-year journey through the history of two continents, accomplished through plenty of hands-on fun, multimedia presentations, and interactive exhibitions (kids will love the mock medieval jousting tournament). Adults will be impressed by the Royal Armouries collection itself, which, in conjunction with Britain's Tower of London, offers a look at British and European history from the 11th to the 20th centuries.

829 West Main St. (502) 753-5663. www.fraziermuseum.org.
Monday–Saturday, 9:00 a.m.–5:00 p.m.; Sunday, noon–5:00 p.m.
Admission: adults, $9; seniors, $7; children, $6.

LOUISVILLE SCIENCE CENTER AND IMAX THEATER

From an Egyptian mummy to an exhibit on human anatomy and physiology, this museum will delight even those who dreaded their high school science class. Permanent exhibits focus on The World Around Us (three ecological galleries — air, land, and sea), The World We Create (a fascinating look at creativity in areas ranging from architecture to transportation), and The World Within Us (guaranteed to give you a better appreciation for the human body).

The center is located in a rehabbed warehouse in the city's museum district and also houses a four-story IMAX theater that shows a variety of films on the natural environment.

727 W. Main St. (502) 561-6100. www.LouisvilleScience.org. Monday–Thursday, 9:30 a.m.–5:00 p.m.; Friday and Saturday, 9:30 a.m.–9:00 p.m.; Sunday, 9:30 a.m.–5:00 p.m. Prices range from $10 to $12 for a museum ticket to $12 to $15 for a combination ticket, which includes both the museum and IMAX.

Other Attractions

LOUISVILLE ZOO

From a lofty position, he reigns over his domain like the noble ruler he is, penetrating eyes taking in the throngs who pass by, one by one, admiring subjects all. He is a male silverback Western lowland gorilla whose ever-shrinking natural habitat is now only a small area of the East Africa countries of Rwanda and Uganda.

It's a long way from the tropical rainforests of East Africa to the bluegrass of Kentucky, but the Western lowland gorillas that hang out in the Louisville Zoo's Gorilla Forest have made themselves at home. Their 9,300-square-foot sanctuary lies at the end of a discovery trail that wends its way through lush tropical growth where sharp-eyed observers can also spot pygmy hippos frolicking in their watering hole and whimsical meerkats and naked mole rats scampering about their earthen dwellings.

In the neighboring African Savannah, visitors become intrepid adventurers in search of the Dark Continent's big game — elephants, rhinos, and lions — as well as zebras and giraffes.

The Indian Ocean may separate the continents of Africa and Australia, but here the two are practically next-door neighbors. After you've had your fill of the veldt, head off to the Outback to visit some of Australia's most recognizable animals — kookaburras, emus, and wallabies. Before leaving "Down Under," be sure to visit Lorikeet Landing, a walk-through aviary in the middle of an Australian station (farm). Lorikeets are a type of parrot indigenous to Australia, and like the human Aussies are brash and bold, with no hesitation in landing on the arms, shoulders, or even heads of visitors. Buy a cup of nectar and you will discover just how little it takes to make a lorikeet love you.

One of the zoo's newest and most popular attractions is "Islands," a three-acre trek into the wilds of Indonesia and the Malay Peninsula with a little bit of the Pacific Rim thrown in for good measure. Designed in typical Indonesian village style, the exhibit features a rich diversity of birds, mammals, and reptiles. Playful

DID YOU KNOW

E.P. Sawyer State Park in Louisville was named for Erbon Powers Sawyer. If that name doesn't ring a bell, perhaps his daughter's will: Diane Sawyer, who began her journalism career doing the weather at a Louisville TV station.

orangutans, elegant Sumatran tigers, and fierce-looking Komodo dragons are all favorite residents of the exhibit.

From the 134 beautifully landscaped acres to more than 1,300 of the rarest animals on earth, the zoo brings the flora and fauna of the world to the center of Louisville.

⬦⬦⬦⬦⬦⬦⬦⬦⬦⬦⬦

**1100 Trevilian Way. (502) 459-2181. www.louisvillezoo.org.
The zoo is open year round, except for Thanksgiving, Christmas,
and New Year's Day; hours change seasonally.
Admission: adults, $11.95; seniors, $9.95; children, $8.50.**

ACTORS THEATRE OF LOUISVILLE

Founded in 1964 and named Kentucky's State Theatre a decade later, Actors is one of America's most consistently innovative professional theater companies. From Moliere and Pirandello to Marsha Norman and John Pielmeier, Shakespeare to Sherlock Holmes, commedia dell'arte to comedies of manners, Tennessee Williams to the theater of the Weimar Republic, it seems there is no genre Actors doesn't do and do extremely well.

The magic begins the moment you walk into the lobby of the Greek Revival building that once housed the Bank of Louisville. Light filters in through a glass-domed cupola. Contemporary art hangs in the corridors. Stylish patrons sip cosmos at the bar or enjoy a pre-theater meal at the lower-level Intermezzo Café. But all this is just a prelude before the curtain goes up on the main act — world-class theater on three separate stages — the 637-seat Pamela Brown Auditorium, the 318-seat Bingham Theatre, and the more intimate 159-seat Victor Jory Theatre, named for the actor who in 1976 started the internationally acclaimed Humana Festival of New American Plays, held every year from February to April.

Since its inception, critics, playwrights, and audiences alike have lauded the festival, making it the country's pre-eminent showcase of new theatrical work. Among the more than 350 plays, representing the work of some 225 playwrights, which have premiered at the festival are the Pulitzer Prize-winning *Crimes of the Heart* and *The Gin Game*. Some 45 Actors Theatre premieres have gone on to be produced on New York stages, and more than 250 are now part of American dramatic literature.

For these efforts, Actors Theatre has been honored with a special Tony Award as an outstanding non-profit resident theater. The list of thespians who have trod its boards reads like a Who's Who of Broadway and Hollywood. They include Kathy Bates, Timothy Busfield, Chris Cooper, Holly Hunter, Julianne Moore, John Turturro, and Stephanie Zimbalist.

With its success in both artistic programming (presenting nearly 600 performances of some 30 productions during its year-round season) and business acumen (it boasts one of the largest per capita subscription audiences and draws more than 200,000 theater-goers annually), Actors is one of America's leading regional theaters.

316 West Main St. (591) 584-1205.
www.actorstheatre.org.

Historic Homes

FARMINGTON

No other house in Kentucky more typifies the elegant Federal style than this 14-room home that served as the center of a 19th-century hemp plantation owned by John and Lucy Speed. The house, completed in 1816, was designed from a plan by Thomas Jefferson and features many of his trademark touches — two octagonal rooms, a hidden stairway, and fanlights between the front and rear halls. However, Jefferson was not the only president to have a Farmington connection; Abraham Lincoln, a friend of the Speeds' son Joshua, spent three weeks here in 1841. The 18-acre site also includes a 19th-century garden, stone springhouse and barn, kitchen, blacksmith shop, apple orchard, museum store, and remodeled carriage house. There is also a permanent exhibit, "Lincoln and Farmington: An Enduring Friendship."

3033 Bardstown Rd. (502) 452-9920. www.historichomes.org/ farmington. Tuesday–Saturday, 10:00 a.m.–4:00 p.m., with tours on the hour. Admission: adults, $9; seniors, $8; children 6–18, $4; 5 and under, free.

LOCUST GROVE

One of the earliest of the area's grand homes is this elegant Georgian-style mansion built in 1790 by William Croghan, who was married to the sister of Louisville's founder, George Rogers Clark. For his time, Croghan certainly had some grandiose ideas as he equipped his frontier residence with a grand ballroom. The site, a National Historic Landmark, is situated on 55 acres of beautifully manicured grounds and features nine outbuildings and a restored garden. The house itself is furnished with period antiques. As it was the final home of George Rogers Clark, whose nephew was explorer William Clark, Locust Grove has been added to the Lewis & Clark National Historic Trail.

561 Blankenbaker La. (502) 897-9845. www.locustgrove.org. Monday–Saturday, 10:00 a.m.–4:30 p.m.; Sunday, 1:00–4:30 p.m. Last tour every day is at 3:15 p.m. Admission: adults, $8; seniors, $7; children, $4.

LOUISVILLE'S GRAND HOTELS — THE SEELBACH AND THE BROWN

If one were to tell tales about Louisville's two grande dames — the Seelbach and the Brown — those tales would amuse, titillate, and scandalize.

At the Seelbach, the tales would reveal how novelist Charles Dickens — apparently not the English gentleman he seemed — was once ejected for a lapse in the hotel's strict code of manners, and how writer F. Scott Fitzgerald's stay in its elegant rooms — sipping Kentucky bourbon and smoking expensive cigars — would later inspire him to use the ballroom as the setting for Tom and Daisy Buchanan's wedding in *The Great Gatsby*.

At the Brown, the whispers would be about how opera diva Lily Pons allowed her pet lion cub to roam freely in her suite and about how Louisville native Victor Mature had a brief stint as an elevator operator before earning fame as a 1950s Hollywood leading man.

The Seelbach, one of America's best examples of the Beaux Arts Baroque style of architecture, began as the dream of two Bavarian brothers, Otto and Louis Seelbach. During its long history the hotel has closed and re-opened several times (the 1905 opening, timed to coincide with the Kentucky Derby, saw the biggest party Louisville had ever thrown, with a five-hour public inspection drawing more than 25,000 visitors), and today flies the Hilton flag.

For more than a century the great and near great, the famous and the infamous have trod the hotel's halls and corridors. Their stays have been both happy — Billy Joel commandeering the piano at the hotel bar and entertaining patrons with an impromptu concert — and sad — the young bride who, eagerly awaiting her new husband in the ballroom to begin their wedding reception, learned of his accidental death on his way to the hotel and, heartbroken, threw herself down an elevator shaft. Today, legend has it that she walks the hotel's halls as the Lady in Blue, eternally mourning her dead bridegroom.

The Seelbach has been a magnet for U.S. presidents (nine of them have stayed here), celebrities, and captains of industry, but its greatest cachet came from its association with less-savory types. In the 1920s, Prohibition made millionaires out of underworld kingpins who were naturally drawn to the most glamorous spots for backroom card games and bootlegged whiskey. In Louisville, this was the Seelbach.

Dutch Schultz and Lucky Luciano were regulars. Cincinnati mobster George Remus, dubbed the "King of the Bootleggers," hung out here, and his charisma so impressed Scott Fitzgerald the writer used him as the inspiration for Jay Gatsby. The Seelbach was also a favorite of Al Capone, Prohibition's most famous gangster, who visited regularly to play blackjack and poker and drink in the Rathskeller. Today, if you dine in the Oak Room, you can sit in the alcove where Capone always sat. The mirror he had sent from Chicago so he could watch his back still hangs in the room.

The Seelbach, though listed on the National Register of Historic Places, has a rival for cachet and elegance in the Brown. In 1922, when Louisville millionaire lumberman and capitalist J. Graham Brown built a $4 million, 15-story hotel at the corner of Fourth and Broadway, it quickly became the city's business and social center. The first "guest" — even before the hotel officially opened, was British Prime Minister David Lloyd George, who, while on a tour of the city, became the first person to sign the register.

Successive guests were equally high profile. Queen Marie of Romania paid a visit in 1926 and was entertained in the Crystal Ballroom, which had been decked out for the occasion with a red carpet and a gold throne on a dais. Even those whose behavior was not quite so regal, nonetheless, misbehaved with flair. Al Jolson, on tour at the nearby Brown Theater, became involved in a bout of fisticuffs in the oh-so-proper English Grill. Far from being abashed at his boorish behavior, Jolson confidently assured fans that his stage make-up would cover the resulting shiner.

The Brown's greatest fame during these early years came not from a star but from a sandwich. In 1923 the hotel drew a thousand people each evening for its dinner dance; afterward, in the wee hours, they would retire to the restaurant for a bite to eat. Deciding that ham and eggs would not do for such a glamorous crowd, then-chef Fred Schmidt created an open-face turkey sandwich with bacon, pimentos, and a delicate mornay sauce. The Hot Brown was born.

If the Seelbach flourished during Prohibition, the Brown faltered. Though Brown defaulted on a loan and his hotel appeared in danger of closing, he managed to keep it open, primarily by appealing to employees to work temporarily without pay.

As if Prohibition and the Depression weren't enough to take the bloom off the Brown's rose, in January 1937 Louisville was deluged when the Ohio River overflowed its banks. The hotel went overnight from being a retreat for the rich to being a refugee camp for the temporarily displaced. More than 1,000 people from the city's lower-lying areas became unexpected (and unpaying) guests for 10 days. There were moments of mirth along with the misery. After the water level rose to three feet on the first floor, the bell captain caught a two-pound fish in the lobby.

If the decade of the '30s was a bust, the '40s were a boom for the Brown. The war years saw two or three trains a day carrying soldiers from nearby Fort Knox to Louisville for R & R. They headed directly to the hotel where they knew they could always find the prettiest girls and the most sympathetic bartenders. The postwar years saw more deals struck in the English Grill than in any boardroom, and Derby night in the Crystal Ballroom was the most important social event of the year.

Today, the Brown, managed by Atlanta-based Camberley Hotel Company, remains a cornerstone in downtown, a fitting tribute to its proud heritage.

The Seelbach Hilton Hotel, 500 Fourth Ave.
(502) 585-3200. www.seelbachhilton.com.
The Camberley Brown Hotel, 335 West Broadway.
(502) 583-1234. www.brownhotel.com.

BELLE OF LOUISVILLE

A century-and-a-half ago, floating palaces with iron lace balconies, sumptuously decorated parlors and staterooms, and whistling calliopes carried well-bred gentlemen, elegant ladies, and riverboat gamblers on an odyssey in search of, respectively, a big adventure, a big catch, and a big score.

Those nostalgic about what life was like on the Mississippi (or in this case, the Ohio) can book passage aboard the *Belle of Louisville* on one of her daily two-hour trips up and down the river (from Memorial Day to Labor Day). A beloved city symbol, the Belle was built in 1914 and remains the oldest operating steam-driven paddlewheeler in the country.

401 W. River Rd. (docked at the foot of Fourth Street).
(502) 574-2992. www.belleoflouisville.org.

INNER BLUEGRASS

Kentucky Department of Tra...

8

Attractions of the Inner Bluegrass

Within an hour's drive of Lexington can be found some of the Bluegrass region's most scenic locations and important sites. From the largest restored Shaker community in the country to a historic Civil War garrison to the folk art capital of the commonwealth, this is an area rich in attractions.

Berea

It is rare that an entire town can be considered an American icon, but Berea falls into a category that includes such places as Williamsburg, Virginia; Salem, Massachusetts; and Deadwood, South Dakota — towns that symbolize a particular slice of American history.

While Williamsburg has colonial history; Salem has witchcraft trials, and Deadwood would be dead without its two most famous citizens, Wild Bill Hickok and Calamity Jane, Berea's fame stems primarily from a unique college.

Nestled in the Cumberland Valley, at the gateway of the Appalachian Mountains, the beautiful tree-shaded campus of Berea College, with its impressive Greek Revival and Federal-style buildings, began as a one-room schoolhouse in 1855 when the Reverend John Fee envisioned an oasis of learning for men and women of all races.

In pre-Civil War Kentucky, where the idea of serious education for women was scoffed at and teaching blacks was against the law, Fee's concept was revolutionary. Fee's passion attracted the attention of Cassius Marcellus Clay, a wealthy landowner and abolitionist who offered Fee a 10-acre homestead on the edge of the mountains if he would take up residence there. Fee agreed, and soon his 13-member anti-slavery church in the community of Berea, named for the biblical town, was doing double duty as a place of worship and a place of learning. He recruited his teachers from the notoriously liberal Oberlin College in Ohio, and Berea soon became known as the "Oberlin of the South."

The Utopian experiment was short-lived, however, when local pro-slavery sympathizers drove Fee and his faculty from Madison County in 1859. The college remained closed during the Civil War years, but in 1865 Fee and his followers returned and with them, Berea College. In 1866-67 the school enrolled 91 white students and 96 black students.

In 1904 the college was dealt another blow when the Kentucky Legislature passed a law prohibiting integrated education, a law that remained in force for nearly half a century. When it was amended in 1950 to allow integration above the high-school level, Berea was the first undergraduate college in Kentucky to welcome black students.

Today Berea College draws students from the southern mountain region of Appalachia, an area the institution has served since 1911 when it amended its admissions policy. Ranked as the top comprehensive college in the South by *U.S. News and World Report*, its mission is to provide a quality liberal arts education, free of charge (students work in the community in lieu of paying tuition). Its motto, "God has made of one blood all people of the earth," has remained unchanged since the school's founding.

KENTUCKY'S ARTS AND CRAFTS CAPITAL

The town of Berea grew around the college, and its students are an integral part of the community. Because they pay no tuition, students are required to work all four years, and they can be found serving mocha lattes at the coffee shop on the town square, manning the desk at the famed Boone Tavern, opened in 1909 and today listed in *America's Historic Inns* (see Chapter 11), and clerking at shops such as the Appalachian Fireside Gallery, Blue Tail Fly, and the Log House Craft Gallery.

The latter are part of a cadre of shops, studios, and galleries that have helped Berea earn the title "Folk Art Capital of Kentucky." Since the opening of Churchill Weavers in 1922, the town has attracted talented artists and artisans from across the commonwealth, and today high-quality folk art is on display in two major areas: College Square and Old Town Artists' Village. The more traditional establishments, such as the Appalachian Fireside Gallery, specializing in decorative pottery and handmade quilts, and the Log House Craft Gallery, Berea's oldest (1917) and largest gallery, are located in College Square, while the Village's more contemporary bent can be seen in the names of the shops: Honeysuckle Vine, Fish Wisdom Beads, Top Drawer Gallery, and I Love My Stuff. The one thing they all have in common, whether traditional or contemporary, is the quality of their products (which translates into prices that are not exactly in the bargain range).

The most recent showcase for Berea's craft heritage is the Kentucky Artisan Center. Within its 25,000 square feet of space can be found superbly crafted glasswork, woodwork, jewelry, woven products, and art work. On Saturdays visitors can get up close and personal with the artists as they watch vases being thrown and glass being blown while listening to the sweet notes of the dulcimer or the click-clack of the weaver's shuttle. In addition to the demonstrations, there are readings and book signings by Kentucky authors as well as art and photography exhibits.

∞:∞◇:∞:◇∞:◇

Berea is 35 miles south of Lexington on Interstate 75.
For information on Berea tourism, call (800) 598-5263
or go to www.berea.com.
The Kentucky Artisan Center is located off I-75 at exit 77.
Open seven days a week (except for Thanksgiving, Christmas,
and New Year's Day) 8:00 a.m.–8:00 p.m.
Craft demonstrations are held on Saturdays, 10:30 a.m.–3:30 p.m.
For information, call (859) 985-5448 or go to
www.kentuckyartisancenter.ky.gov.

Danville

PERRYVILLE BATTLEFIELD STATE HISTORIC SITE

The explosion of a cannon sends birds soaring skyward, their fear-laced shrieks competing with the moans of mortally wounded soldiers, many of them barely past adolescence. Across the rural landscape the two columns advance toward each other, their tattered and blood-soaked gray and blue uniforms sad symbols of a nation divided. Muskets and bayonets are leveled, shots ring out, and the killing fields surrounding Perryville are littered with corpses.

October 1862 at the height of the Civil War in Kentucky? Try any modern-day October when "Union" and "Confederate" forces, along with thousands of spectators, gather on the battlefield for the annual re-enactment of the commonwealth's most important Civil War battle. They travel back to the early days of the

War Between the States, assuming the identities of the Armies of the Ohio and Mississippi, under the leadership of Generals Don Carlos Buell and Braxton Bragg, respectively.

They re-enact two key segments of the battle in which 40,000 men fought and 7,500 were killed or wounded, one of the worst per-hour casualty numbers of the war, and where, during two days of fierce fighting, the fate of Kentucky — and some historians argue, the entire nation — hung in the balance.

Today visitors, looking at the peaceful green hills and valleys outside of Danville, find it hard to imagine the ferocity of the October 7–8 battle, and are perplexed as to why the relatively obscure (except to historians and Civil War scholars) Battle of Perryville is considered the watershed battle of the war, rather than the better known battles of Antietam, Bull Run, and Gettysburg. Its importance, however, cannot be overstated.

For what was at stake that autumn afternoon was, basically, the fate of the nation. A Confederate victory would have severed the Union supply lines along the Ohio River, making it difficult, if not impossible, for the Army of the Republic to supply its troops in the Deep South. If Kentucky were to be taken by the Rebels, it would have meant thousands of fresh recruits for the Confederate army, not to mention a steady supply of horses from central Kentucky.

The battle did indeed live up to advance expectations. After fierce fighting, with both sides gaining ground and then losing it, the Confederates won a tactical victory, with Sam Watkins and his First Tennessee battalion saving the day. But if the Rebel army won a tactical victory, it suffered a strategic defeat. The relentless pressure from the Union troops forced Bragg to withdraw from the state, ending hopes of a Confederate Kentucky. Never again would the Confederate Army, other than through sporadic cavalry raids, have a presence in Kentucky.

1825 Battlefield Rd., Perryville. (859) 332-8631. www.parks.ky.gov/findparks/histparks/pb/. Administered by the Department of Parks, the battlefield has some 45 interpretive signs at important points along the self-guided trails. As most of these trails are in open meadow with little shade, wear a hat and take plenty of water if you are visiting in the summer.

A museum has educational displays of artifacts and other memorabilia. Not far from the museum, you will find two monuments — one honoring the Confederacy, erected in 1902, the other, the Union, erected in 1931.

CONSTITUTION SQUARE STATE HISTORIC SITE

This square block in downtown Danville is the birthplace of the state of Kentucky. In the late 18th century, the square's buildings included a courthouse and a meetinghouse, but it was in Grayson's Tavern where influential citizens first met in 1784 to begin framing a constitution that would separate what is now Kentucky from Virginia. The process took eight years and it wasn't until June 1, 1792, that Kentucky entered the Union as the 15th state.

The Governor's Circle in the square's northwest quadrant pays tribute to all of the commonwealth's governors, beginning with the first, Isaac Shelby. The monument's centerpiece is a statue of a statesman, smartly turned out in a well-tailored frock coat, shaking hands with a frontiersman in buckskins, with the state motto, "United We Stand, Divided We Fall."

Surrounding Constitution Square are a few of the original buildings, including the post office, which when built in the 1790s was the first post office west of the Alleghenies, and replicas of the courthouse, jail, and meetinghouse.

134 South Second St., Danville. (859) 239-7089.
www.parks.ky.gov/findparks/histparks/cs/

MCDOWELL HOUSE & APOTHECARY SHOP

If you leave Constitution Square and walk across Second Street, you will find a modest white-frame dwelling in the Federal style of architecture common during the late 18th and early 19th centuries. This is no ordinary house, but rather the Ephraim McDowell House & Apothecary. Now a museum, the house was where McDowell, a Scottish-trained physician, gained a place in Kentucky lore by performing in 1809 the first successful surgery to remove an ovarian tumor (on a woman who endured the operation without benefit of anesthesia). Dr. McDowell went on to become world renowned in abdominal surgical techniques; the patient, one Jane Crawford, alas, faded into semi-obscurity (although there have been several plays and stories written about her). Tours of the house, apothecary, and garden are available. www.mcdowellhouse.com.

Frankfort

STATE CAPITOL COMPLEX

First on any Frankfort visitor's agenda should be a tour of the Capitol and grounds. From its imposing location at the end of flower-lined Capitol Avenue to the beautiful floral clock on the premises to the elegant Beaux Arts style of the building itself, the Capitol complex is worth a visit.

Stand in the Capitol rotunda and gaze up 171 feet to the dome modeled after France's Hotel des Invalides, the Paris burial place of Napoleon Bonaparte. The grand staircase also has a French flair, being modeled after that of the Paris Opera House. Other embellishments, however, are strictly Kentucky, from the bronze statues of Abraham Lincoln, Jefferson Davis, Henry Clay, and other notable native sons to the colorful murals that depict such scenes as Daniel Boone getting his first look at Kentucky and the Treaty of Sycamore Shoals, which led to the purchase of land from the Cherokees.

You'll want to see the House and Senate chambers (open to the public when the General Assembly is not in session) and the imposing state reception room (again with a French twist — inspired by Marie Antoinette's drawing room at Versailles), but you also won't want to miss the First Ladies in Miniature, a collection of dolls showcasing every first lady in her inaugural ball gown. Note: Phyllis George, then wife of former Governor John Y. Brown, might have been Miss America, but the real glamour girl among the first femmes was Ida Lee Willis, the 46th first lady in a slinky number that wasn't exactly characteristic of the times.

Free tours are offered Monday to Friday. Guided tours are every 30 minutes, 8:30 a.m.–3:00 p.m. Hours for self-guided tours are 8:00 a.m.–4:00 p.m.

Across from the new Capitol Building is the Governor's Mansion, completed in 1914, and whose architecture mimics that of Marie Antoinette's Petit Trianon at Versailles.

The mansion is open to visitors on Tuesdays and Thursdays from 9:00 a.m.–11:00 a.m. Tours must be booked through the State Capitol office by calling (502) 564-3449.

Finally, don't miss the lovely Floral Clock, located just behind the Capitol. Its flower face is composed of seasonal plantings. At 34 feet tall, the clock has a 530-pound minute hand and a

420-pound second hand.

Once you have seen the New Capitol building (built from 1906 to 1910), you'll probably want to wander over to the Old State Capitol on West Broadway. Designed by Lexington architect Gideon Shryock, who was also responsible for Transylvania University's Morrison Hall on the Lexington campus, it was a bold statement for its time (the early 19th century). Almost an exact duplicate of the Temple of Minerva in Greece, it was the first building west of the Appalachians to be designed in Greek Revival style. If imitation is the sincerest form of flattery, it should be noted that Shryock's design was so lauded that it inspired the building of the state capitols of Illinois, Ohio, Tennessee, Arkansas, and Mississippi.

Of particular interest are the freestanding circular stone staircase below the dome, the House and Senate chambers (complete with brass spittoons beneath the desks), and the statue of William Goebel, who has the distinction of being the only U.S. governor assassinated while in office (former Louisiana governor Huey Long was a U.S. Senator when he was gunned down in Baton Rouge's old Capitol building).

As the Goebel story goes, the 1899 election for governor had been fiercely contested, with both parties accusing the other of skullduggery and vote rigging. On January 30, 1900, the victorious Goebel was on his way to the legislative session when he was shot by an assassin hiding in the Secretary of State's office in the Capitol annex. Goebel lingered for four days before succumbing to his wounds, long enough to be sworn in and to request oysters shipped from New Orleans for his last meal.

HISTORIC HOMES

Frankfort has so many historic homes it is difficult to know where to start, but arguably the most important is Liberty Hall. Built by

John Brown (not the John Brown of song whose body lies a-moldering in the grave, but the John Brown who was one of the state's first two senators), the house has a number of distinctions: The first Sunday school west of the Alleghenies was held in its front parlor; the dining room saw three presidents (James Monroe, Zachary Taylor, and Andrew Jackson) and the Marquis de Lafayette sit down to dinner, and, even after several centuries the ghost of a family member known as the "gray lady" still makes an occasional appearance.

The home is open to the public Tuesday–Saturday, with four tours daily at 10:30 a.m., noon, 1:30 p.m., and 3:00 p.m. The ticket price of $4 for adults, $3 for seniors, and $1 for students and children gets you into both Liberty Hall and the neighboring Orlando Brown House. Strolling through Liberty Hall's beautiful gardens, which slope down to the Kentucky River, is free.

202 Wilkinson St. (502) 227-2560. www.libertyhall.org.

THOMAS D. CLARK CENTER FOR KENTUCKY HISTORY

A combination ticket ($4 for adults; $2 for ages 6–18; free for children 5 and under) will get you into the Old Capitol building and this museum, named in honor of one of Kentucky's most beloved icons, the late University of Kentucky history professor who, even after hitting the century mark in 2003, was still active as a historian, speaker, and writer.

In this facility visitors can tour the state from prehistoric times to the present, taking in interactive exhibits including a Native American village and a simulated coal mine and company store. Hours for both museums are 10:00 a.m.–5:00 p.m., Tuesday–Saturday.

100 West Broadway. www.history.ky.gov/

CAPITAL CITY MUSEUM

Anyone who thinks museums have to be stuffy and scholarly hasn't been to this small gem. Here are some of the interesting tidbits you can glean from a visit:

The 1825 murder of Kentucky solicitor general Solomon P. Sharp by the husband of his former lover inspired Edgar Allan Poe's only attempt at writing a play — his unfinished *Politian*.

Bibb lettuce was developed by amateur horticulturist John B. Bibb in his Wapping Street backyard in 1865.

Vest Lindsay House, also on Wapping Street, was the boyhood home of George Graham Vest, who might not be remembered for his political achievements as a U.S. Senator from Missouri, but who should be acknowledged for coining the phrase, "a dog is man's best friend."

General James Wilkinson, known as Silky Wilky to most and Agent 13 to a few, may have been a spy for the Spanish government, but he is also given credit for developing Frankfort as a port for shipping goods to New Orleans.

In a sort of reversal of the Fleet Street barber *Sweeney Todd*, whose victims were his customers, Frankfort had a serial murderer in the 1870s who preyed on butchers.

**325 Ann St. (502) 696-9127. Monday–Saturday,
10:00 a.m.–4:00 p.m. Admission is free.**

KENTUCKY VIETNAM VETERANS MEMORIAL

Designed as a large modern sundial overlooking a granite plaza, the memorial honors the memory of 1,100 Kentuckians killed or missing in action during the Vietnam War. The design concept is such that the gnomon, the pin of the sundial, casts its shadow on the name of each veteran on the anniversary of his death.

Coffee Tree Rd. www.kyvietnammemorial.net.

REBECCA RUTH CANDIES

It's a chocolate factory that would make even Willy Wonka proud. The modest white cottage with red shutters and awning in the shadow of the state capitol seems an unlikely setting to house one of Kentucky's most popular exports, but once inside the doors there's no doubt that here, chocolate rules: horse heads fashioned of white and dark chocolate, raspberry jellies, caramels, pecan blondies, and some 125 other types. But in this chocolate empire, one reigns supreme. Rebecca Ruth (named for the two schoolteachers, Ruth Hanley and Rebecca Gooch, who founded the company in 1919) was the first ever to produce candy made with 100 proof bourbon whiskey, and even though the maximum used is 5 percent, the small bonbons known as "bourbon balls" still pack a mighty wallop. Bourbon ball aficionados insist that Rebecca Ruth's are fit for the gods.

Public tours, which cost 50 cents, are offered Monday–Saturday, 9:00 a.m.–4:30 p.m. on a walk-in basis.

112 E. Second St.

(800) 444-3766. www.rebeccaruth.com.

SHAKER VILLAGE OF PLEASANT HILL

It's a scene that could be reproduced on a Hallmark greeting card — 2,900 acres of unspoiled, undulating farmland ending at the stark palisades of the Kentucky River. The rolling hills, frequently softened by early morning river mist, are broken by stream-laced woodlands, 35 miles of hiking trails, and 34 buildings dating back nearly 200 years and bordered by immaculate white picket fences. Men and women in period costume labor at the loom or the spinning wheel, in the communal farm, or in the herb garden. The sound of voices raised in a hymn drifts from the Meeting House, while the aroma of home-cooked food wafts from the Trustees' Office.

Visitors could be forgiven for thinking they had stumbled into a time warp, especially considering they're only 20 miles from Lexington. This is Shaker Village of Pleasant Hill, the largest restored Shaker community in the United States and the first site in the country to be designated in its entirety as a National Historic Landmark.

Today Shaker Village is one of Kentucky's most popular tourist attractions, but for 105 years — from 1805, when it was founded, to 1910, when it closed its doors as an active religious community — it was home to the United Society of Believers in Christ's Second Appearing, or — due to their ecstatic, animated movements during worship services — "Shakers."

The Shaker movement began in England at the end of the 18th century and quickly found a home in the New World, first in New England, and then in the frontier areas of Kentucky, Indiana, Illinois, and Ohio. In common with the Quakers and Amish, Shakers believed in pacifism, environmentalism, and non-materialism.

They also shared a belief in the equality of the sexes, but unlike the other two sects, they practiced celibacy, relying on converts to sustain their communities.

At Pleasant Hill, visitors get an insight into the Shakers' many talents: spiritual music (they wrote more than 20,000 hymns), architectural skills (the dual cantilevered staircases in the Trustees' Office spiral up three stories with no external support), and the quality of their furniture, still prized by collectors today. What is perhaps most remarkable is that while the last Shaker departed the village a century ago, nearly every important building remains, thanks to a grassroots conservation and restoration effort that began in 1961. Today visitors can spend a day or several days exploring the village and immersing themselves in the culture of one of the most unusual and progressive religious sects ever founded.

The self-guided tour includes 14 original buildings, highlights of which are the 40-room Centre Family Dwelling with its fine collection of original Shaker furniture and craft objects, and the excellent Shaker Life exhibit located in the lower level of the East Family Dwelling. Throughout the village, costumed interpreters talk about Shaker life and work at tasks associated with Pleasant Hill a century-and-a-half ago. Demonstrations of crafts such as broom making, spinning, basket weaving, and coopering (barrel and cask repairing) as well as discussions of Shaker theology are held several times daily. A few of the village's activities are seasonal; an authentic sternwheeler, the *Dixie Belle*, does five trips a day on the Kentucky River from late April to early October, and during that same time period Shaker music is performed four times daily in the 1820 Meeting House.

For better insight into Shaker life, get off the beaten path. Wander along the 1837 turnpike, now a nearly deserted country lane that leads to the cemetery, the remains of a gristmill, and an ancient springhouse, or marvel at the 25 miles of stone fences, an engineering feat peculiar to Kentucky's Bluegrass region. The fences are drywall, with stones stacked together without benefit of any type of mortar.

Because it is so close to Lexington, some visitors opt for a day trip to Shaker Village. However, increasingly, more and more are choosing to stay overnight to take advantage of the full spectrum of what the facility has to offer. The 81 guest rooms are spread throughout the village in 15 of the restored buildings where the Shakers once lived and worked. While each room is furnished with Shaker-inspired reproduction furniture, handwoven rugs, and hand-loomed coverlets, they also have modern conveniences and have been listed in the *Zagat World's Top Hotels, Resorts & Spas* (see Chapter 11).

But even if you don't stay overnight, you should not leave Pleasant Hill without enjoying a meal (breakfast, lunch, or dinner) in the candlelit dining rooms of the Trustees' Office. Locals and visitors alike flock here to enjoy such traditional fare as tomato celery soup; homemade coleslaw (the best I've ever eaten); cornbread sticks; pan-fried catfish; country ham; and Shaker lemon pie, filled with tart, paper-thin slivers of lemon.

Walking the tree-shaded paths at Pleasant Hill, one can't help but be reminded of the Shakers' belief that here, in the Kentucky Bluegrass, they had achieved an earthly Utopia.

〰〰〰〰〰〰〰

3501 Lexington Rd., Harrodsburg.
(800) 734-5611. www.shakervillageky.org.
Open daily except for December 24 and 25;
April–October, 9:30 a.m.–5:30 p.m.; winter hours vary.

OLD FORT HARROD STATE PARK

Fort Boonesborough may get the bulk of attention due to its connection with the romantic exploits of Daniel Boone, but Fort Harrod has the distinction of being Kentucky's first permanent settlement, having been founded by pioneer James Harrod in 1774, a year before Boone founded his namesake settlement.

While he never got the place in history that was awarded to Boone, Harrod had an equally fascinating, albeit tragic, life (his brother and son were both killed by Indians) and a mysterious end that could be the subject of a television docudrama (after the torture and burning at the stake of his son, Harrod began to disappear on increasingly longer hunting trips; after one such trip in 1792, he vanished and was never heard from again).

Old Fort Harrod has undergone reconstruction, and the heavy timber stockade walls encircle cabins and blockhouses that were built around a spring bubbling from a nearby hillside. Costumed craftspeople perform pioneer tasks such as weaving, woodworking, and blacksmithing, while others tend to farm animals and gardens.

Other points of interest are the original log cabin where the marriage of Thomas and Nancy (Abraham Lincoln's parents) took place in 1806; the oldest cemetery west of the Appalachians; a federal monument dedicated to the exploration of the Northwest Territories by Kentuckian George Rogers Clark; and a giant Osage orange tree estimated to have been there when the fort was built.

⚬⚬⚬⚬⚬⚬⚬⚬⚬⚬⚬

100 South College St., Harrodsburg. (859) 734-3314.
www.parks.ky.gov. March–October, 9:00 a.m.–5:00 p.m. and
November–March, 9:00 a.m.–4:30 p.m.
Closed on weekends December–February.

Midway/Versailles

One of the Bluegrass region's most charming towns, Midway is a magnet for visitors who come not just from Lexington, about 15 miles away, but from as far afield as Louisville, Cincinnati, and Indianapolis to shop its boutiques and sample the fare at restaurants that would do credit to a city much larger than Midway's 1,700 people.

Midway got its start in 1831 as the first town in Kentucky to be established by a railroad (it got its name from being the midpoint between Lexington and Frankfort on the Lexington & Ohio Railroad route). Its history includes guerilla raids by Confederate general John Hunt Morgan and the notorious raider Sue Mundy; occasional sightings of outlaws Frank and Jesse James, whose mother was born at Offutt-Cole Tavern, located a few miles south of town at Nugents Crossing; and a visit by General George Armstrong Custer, on the lookout for prime equine stock for both the U.S. Army and his own breeding operation.

Today its Victorian-style buildings, painted in ice cream sherbet colors and lining both sides of the railroad track, house unique shops such as Celtic Trends, Eagles' Nest Gallery, Damselfly, and Historic Midway Museum Store, and fine dining restaurants such as Bistro La Belle, Heirloom, and the nearby Holly Hill Inn.

IRISH ACRES ANTIQUES

Imagine a place where staid Victorian drawing room meets 1930s Hollywood over-the-top glamour; where New England blueblood Brahmin rubs elbows with Appalachian mountain folk; where elegant French provincial co-exists with cozy English cottage chic. If you are thinking you would only find such a place in

London, Paris, New York, or New Orleans, then you haven't been to Nonesuch.

Nonesuch is 20 minutes from Lexington, in the heart of Thoroughbred country. With little more than a gas station, a country store, and a few scattered residences, it is the last place you might expect to discover a world-class antique store and restaurant.

But that's just what you find at Irish Acres, a rehabbed red brick building with white columns, which, despite its antebellum appearance, dates back to the Depression era. Built in 1936, it once functioned as the Nonesuch elementary school.

In rooms where children once learned their ABCs, shoppers now learn the ABCs of antique buying — how to tell the difference between a French Empire and a Prudent Mallard four-poster bed, how to distinguish Wedgewood china from Spode, how to tell if that exquisite cut glass cocktail shaker is Art Deco or Art Nouveau. Overseeing their education are the owners, the person-

DID YOU KNOW

Kentucky Colonels are as much a part of the commonwealth as the Kentucky Derby. Originated by Isaac Shelby, the state's first governor, to honor all those who served in the regiment he commanded during the War of 1812, today's Honorable Order of Kentucky Colonels have no official status, serving instead as goodwill ambassadors for the commonwealth. Some notable colonels include Kentucky natives Harlan Sanders, Muhammad Ali and Johnny Depp as well as some unlikely colonels — Winston Churchill and Pope John Paul II. In fact, not being alive didn't preclude the selection of one Colonel: Songwriter Stephen Foster was given a posthumous commission.

able sister act of Jane DeLauter and Emilie McCauley. The sisters deftly manage an "upstairs/downstairs" situation, with Jane handling the upstairs — 32,000 square feet of space on two floors, while Emilie presides over The Glitz, the cellar restaurant that has to be seen to be believed.

Irish Acres has an array of furniture, art, silver, crystal, glassware, jewelry, clothing, Christmas ornaments, and other collectibles, artfully arranged in some 60 small showrooms or vignettes — a French sitting room next to an English bedroom adjoining an early American dining room. Irish Acres' merchandise is eclectic, with museum-quality items from four continents, but don't let that scare you. The merchandise appeals to any taste at prices to match any pocketbook. You can pick up a pair of vintage earrings or a beautifully crafted Christmas ornament for $20, or you can walk out with a 200-year-old mahogany corner cupboard with shell carvings for $38,500.

If the antiques display elicits "oooohhhhs" and "aaaahhhhs," The Glitz, one floor down, is nothing short of breathtaking. A color scheme of silver, black, mauve, and pink, and a décor featuring black and silver butterflies, smoky mirrors, gauzy drapery, and hundreds of twinkling lights, gives it such an other-world feeling that you expect Fred and Ginger to waltz through at any moment. It so resembles a 1940s Hollywood movie set that it's hard to believe it was once the school cafeteria.

On any given day the movie-set scenario is enhanced by tables filled with ladies (and more than a few gents) who lunch. Many come dressed for the part, decked out in hats and gloves, and engaging in witty repartee that would have been worthy of Dorothy Parker in her Round Table days.

The restaurant's three-course menu changes every two weeks. The flute of spiced apple punch that precedes every meal comes from a family recipe, and many of the menu items — country ham, farmhouse cheeses, and luscious strawberries — are definitely Kentucky Proud. But whatever you order, don't leave without trying The Glitz's signature dessert, the Nonesuch Kiss, a meringue shell filled with a scoop of coffee ice cream and topped with hot fudge, sliced almonds, and whipped cream.

Fords Mill Rd., Nonesuch. (859) 873-7235. www.irishacresgallery.com. Tuesday–Saturday, 10:00 a.m.–5:00 p.m., from mid-March through December. Open for lunch on the same days. The three-course lunch is $20 and reservations are essential.

Nicholasville

CAMP NELSON HERITAGE PARK

The land — some 400 acres of sprawling countryside above the palisades of the Kentucky River 20 miles south of Lexington — is quiet, the only sound an errant breeze ruffling the leaves on the trees. But in 1863 it was alive with the sounds of timber being hammered into buildings, anvils struck, ammunition tested, and soldiers drilled.

During the Civil War, this landscape — now ghostly in its vast emptiness — was the site of an important Union quartermaster depot, established as a garrison and supply center for the Army of the Ohio in its campaigns in east Tennessee, central and eastern Kentucky, and southwestern Virginia. For two years its strategic location succeeded in keeping Confederate troops at bay, and its seemingly impregnable fortifications discouraged even the guerilla tactics of General John Hunt Morgan, the "Thunderbolt of the Confederacy," who decided it prudent not to attempt one of his famous raids.

Camp Nelson is also known for being the site of Kentucky's largest (and the nation's third-largest) recruitment and training camp for African-American troops. More than 10,000 slaves gained freedom here, escaping from plantations farther south to enlist in the Union army, where they became known as the U.S. Colored Troops, fighting alongside pro-Union white troops from eastern Kentucky and eastern Tennessee.

Their emancipation helped pave the way for Camp Nelson's second historical contribution — serving as the instrument for slavery's fatal blow in Kentucky. Upon receiving their freedom, many of the soldiers sent for their families to join them in the hope they also would be freed or at least escape the plantations. Thus began Camp Nelson's second phase as the state's largest African-American refugee camp, where at the height of its activity it sheltered nearly 3,000 refugees — most of them wives and children of the U.S. Colored Troops — living in hastily built shanties.

While Camp Nelson's role as a fortification and recruitment center was well thought out — with nine forts, 300 buildings, and 20 large warehouses holding rations, uniforms, weapons, and equipment — its role as a refugee camp remained unresolved, at least until the summer of 1864.

That was the year that General Speed Fry, the camp commander, began his diaspora — expelling black refugees and cooperating with slave owners by returning their "property." This continued practically unnoticed until a bitterly cold day in the autumn when 400 refugees were forced out of camp. Before the order could be countermanded, 102 had died of exposure and disease. The political uproar that ensued led to the 1865 Congressional Act that freed the families of recruits and established a home for the refugees.

By the end of the war, Camp Nelson had outlived its usefulness and the military began closing it down. By June 1866 it had been abandoned. Most of the buildings were sold for their lumber and quickly dismantled, and the Oliver Perry Mansion, known as the "White House," which had been commandeered for use as officers' quarters, was returned to the owners.

Camp Nelson has been called "the best preserved Civil War depot in the country," with 408 of its original 4,000 acres intact. The White House has been meticulously restored and a series of interpretative trails educates visitors on the significant role the camp played. But perhaps nowhere does Camp Nelson come more alive than in the burial place of its dead. On a rolling hill overlooking the palisades lie the remains of some 4,000 Civil War soldiers, including 600 U.S. Colored Troops, and 1,600 more who died while living in the camp. Many of the graves bear no inscription, but the stark white markers speak more eloquently than words ever could.

Camp Nelson Heritage Park is off US 27 (park entrance is off the Danville Pike). Admission is free, and White House tours are Wednesday–Saturday, 10:00 a.m.–4:00 p.m. www.campnelson.org.

Paris

CANE RIDGE MEETING HOUSE

Located a few miles outside of Paris, this is believed to be the largest one-room log structure in North America. Erected in 1791 as a meetinghouse for a Presbyterian congregation, it was the site of the largest camp revival on the American frontier. In August 1801, nearly 30,000 worshippers arrived on foot, by horseback, or by wagon, all in search of salvation. Over the course of six days, they listened as preachers took to the stump, orating with the fervor of the early New England Puritans.

Cane Ridge's second milestone occurred in 1804 when its preacher, Barton Warren Stone, led his congregation away from the rigidity imposed by Presbyterianism and into the kinder, gentler Disciples of Christ denomination. The original log church is still there but now sheltered by a limestone structure.

<hr>

Go north on Paris's Main Street (US 68) and then east on US Highway 460 to 537 North. Follow 537 for about five-and-a-half miles and you will see the shrine on the left side of the road. April– October, 9:00 a.m.–5:00 p.m., Monday–Saturday, and 1:00 p.m.–5:00 p.m. on Sunday. Admission is free, but donations are accepted. (859) 987-5350. www.caneridge.org.

DUNCAN TAVERN

The imposing limestone structure on High Street in downtown Paris was built in 1788 by Revolutionary War officer Major Joseph Duncan, and during its heyday hosted such distinguished wayfarers as Henry Clay, Samuel Adams, Daniel Boone, and Simon Kenton. Hopefully, Clay and Adams got better accommodations than Boone and Kenton, who, as the story goes, had to share a bed with a board to separate them because of the tavern's habitual overcrowding.

Following Duncan Tavern's $400,000 renovation in 2004, its blue ash floors, high ceilings, and spacious windows are again on display as the state headquarters for the Daughters of the American Revolution, who have opened it for tours and special events.

<hr>

323 High St. (859) 987-1788.

Richmond

FORT BOONESBOROUGH

Sunshine dapples the logs of the cabins and throws shadows across the central common ground of the fort. A blacksmith, sweat trickling down his face, labors over his forge; a girl, dressed in simple homespun frock, totes a pail of water; and a group of men and women, some decked out in colonial finery and others in buckskins, are deep in conversation. The only clues a casual observer has that this is not 1775 and the beginning of the Kentucky frontier are an off-duty colonial officer puffing on a cigarette, a pioneer woman pulling a cell phone from her apron, and a group of rambunctious school children on a field trip attempting to scale the fort's walls.

This is Fort Boonesborough, Kentucky's second-oldest settlement (after Fort Harrod) and its most famous. For here, among the crude log dwellings roam the ghosts of Daniel Boone, Simon Kenton, and Richard Henderson, legendary names in the state's pioneer history. Fort Boonesborough today may be a Kentucky State Park and National Historic Landmark, and the "pioneers" costumed re-enactors, but in the late 18th century the rude fort was a bastion of civilization on a bloody frontier.

In spring 1775, Boone and his party reached the lofty palisades of the Kentucky River and decided it was as good a spot as any for a permanent settlement (see Chapter 1). When the frontier pushed farther west, the fort was abandoned and remained a neglected remnant of the commonwealth's pioneer past. In addition to the general deterioration over time, half of the original fort washed away during the 1905-06 construction of a lock on the river.

In 1974 the state began a reconstruction effort without the aid of blueprints to determine the fort's exact location. For more than a decade, visitors, enamored of the legend of Daniel Boone and his brave settlers, were convinced that they trod on hallowed ground. It wasn't until 1987 that an archaeological survey dig determined that the current reconstruction is actually half a mile from the original fort's location.

No matter. Despite the half-mile distance between the original and the reconstruction, Fort Boonesborough provides the modern-day visitor with a window to life on the Kentucky frontier.

<hr />

4375 Boonesborough Rd., Richmond. (859) 527-3131. www.parks.ky.gov/findparks/recparks/fb/. Open seven days a week, 9:00 a.m.–5:30 p.m.
Admission: adults, $7; children 6 to 12, $5; under 6, free.

WHITE HALL

The imposing red brick mansion sits atop a hill just outside Richmond — a fitting palace for the American royalty who called it home for nearly a century. White Hall, the Italianate-style villa filled with heirloom and period furnishings, is today a Kentucky historic site, and while it may be praised for its elegant architecture and impeccable interior design, it is best known for its fascinating former resident.

Cassius Marcellus Clay wore many hats during his long life (born in 1810, he lived to be 93) — firebrand Transylvania student, lawyer, politician, radical emancipationist, newspaper editor, dueler and brawler extraordinaire, foreign emissary, victim of scandal, and friend of presidents and czars. Most of these roles were played out with White Hall's elegant parlors, dining rooms, and boudoirs as the stage.

The sheer size of White Hall — 44 rooms and three floors —

surprises most first-time visitors until they learn the mansion is actually two houses in one. The first, known as Clermont, was built by Clay's father, General Green Clay, in 1798 when Kentucky was still part of Virginia and the general was a member of that state's assembly; the second, called White Hall, was added in the 1860s by Cassius, who became known as "the Lion of White Hall."

With good reason. If these walls could talk, what tales they would tell. No doubt they would tell about how Clay, age 33 and already a fierce opponent of slavery, was set upon by a hired assassin and shot in the chest. Though seriously wounded, he used his Bowie knife (still on display) to cut off the attacker's nose. Fast-forward nearly half a century, and they would tell of how Cassius, age 89, would engage in his last fight. Dressed in his nightshirt, he was reading in the library when three men broke in through the sun porch. Cassius shot the first man, who died on the library floor, and stabbed the second, who made it as far as the ice house before succumbing. The third man, exhibiting more brains than bravado, beat a hasty retreat.

White Hall was the scene of many of Clay's triumphs. The china in the dining room is part of a 104-piece set that he used to entertain while serving eight years as Minister to Russia; an upstairs bedroom was used by Clay's daughter Laura, a prominent suffragette and the first woman ever to receive a vote for a presidential nomination (at the 1920 Democratic National Convention); and in the third-floor hallway is a glass case displaying the *True American*, the newspaper Clay started when other papers refused to publish his anti-slavery views.

But it was also the scene of many of his peccadilloes. The drawing room must have echoed with the heated arguments of Clay and his first wife, Mary Jane, when, upon his return from Russia, he discovered that she had not only spent the $8,000 he had left her to refurbish the house, but an additional $22,000. For her part, she was more than a little suspicious of the young boy that her husband had "adopted" during his stay at the Russian court. Despite a marriage of 45 years, Clay divorced her in 1878.

The scandal with Mary Jane paled in comparison to the furor caused when 84-year-old Clay took as his second wife Dora Richardson, all of 15 at the time of their marriage. From the first-floor entrance, Clay, armed with a loaded cannon, fought off a posse sent to rescue Dora, believing she was being held against her will.

While most of White Hall reflects the life of Cassius Clay, the man, the third-floor hallway reflects the life of Cassius Clay, the American legend. An emancipator rather than an abolitionist, who believed that slaves should be freed not at any cost but through legal methods, he used his newspaper to give voice to his beliefs. In an exhibition area, issues of the paper are positioned next to the brass cannon he purchased and loaded with glass and nails to protect himself and his employees from outraged neighbors who considered him, at best, an eccentric, and at worst, a traitor. The final display case contains Clay's artillery, from the sword he wore in the Mexican War to his weapon of choice, the Bowie knife.

Cassius Clay was a Kentucky and an American icon, and his remarkable story unfolds at White Hall.

⊹⊹⊹⊹⊹⊹⊹

500 White Hall Shrine Rd., off I-75 at Exit 95 in Richmond.
(859) 623-9178. www.parks.ky.gov.
April–September seven days a week,
9:00 a.m.–4:00 p.m.; September–October, five days a week,
and November–March by appointment only.
Admission: adults, $6; children 6–12, $3; under 6, free.

Kentucky Department of Trav

OUTER BLUEGRASS

Attractions of the Outer Bluegrass

Using Louisville as your base, you can take in a number of the commonwealth's major sites. You can taste bourbon at one of the area's distilleries or bourbon fudge at — of all places — a Trappist monastery. You can pay homage to the nation's 16th president by visiting his birthplace in Hodgenville or you can savor the mystique of the Old South with a visit to one of the state's most iconic structures — Federal Hill Plantation, better known as My Old Kentucky Home.

Bardstown

MY OLD KENTUCKY HOME STATE PARK

Except for its imposing location — atop a hill surrounded by a grove of magnolias and elm trees — the three-story red brick house doesn't immediately stand out. Its unpretentious, almost Spartan exterior is typical of the Georgian-style architecture in vogue in the late 18th and early 19th centuries, before the term "plantation" became defined by the white-columned, Tara-like mansions of the Deep South. Certainly, at first glance, nothing about the structure would lead the observer to conclude it is one of the most famous houses in America.

Yet, that's just what Federal Hill is.

The residence of a prominent Kentuckian, Judge John Rowan, Federal Hill might have been just another stately home of its era (construction was started in 1795 and completed in 1818), except for one deciding factor. Judge Rowan, who served on both the Kentucky Court of Appeals and in the United States Senate, entertained some of the most influential men of his day. His soirées were attended by the likes of Henry Clay and Aaron Burr, while the house became a regular rest stop for President Andrew Jackson (who napped on the settee in the hall) on his trips between the White House and The Hermitage, his plantation in Nashville. But it was a relative from Pittsburgh, a young man by the name of Stephen Collins Foster, who may or may not have — depending on the story — paid a visit to the Rowan family in 1852 that ensured the house its place in history — in this case, musical history.

As the story goes, Foster was so moved by the grace and charm of the house and the lifestyle of antebellum Kentucky that he penned what has arguably become the most famous state anthem — "My Old Kentucky Home." For a century and a half, the plaintive words of longing from someone far, far away for his homestead have brought tears to the eyes of Kentuckians at events ranging from the Kentucky Derby to University of Kentucky football and basketball games. In 1928 the state legislature voted to make "My Old Kentucky Home" the commonwealth's official song.

The sun is still shining brightly on My Old Kentucky Home, thanks to a nearly $1 million renovation. The house's exterior has retained its elegant, classical appearance; the formal gardens remain the same, as do the outdoor kitchen, carriage house, and Judge Rowan's law office, where his law classes were interrupted by "frequent mint julep breaks."

Clockwise from top, young Thoroughbreds enjoying a spring day; a statue of the late 1977 Triple Crown winner Seattle Slew at Three Chimneys Farm; the entrance to world-famous Calumet Farm

Clockwise from above, Churchill Downs;
2009 Kentucky Derby winner Mine That
Bird; Keeneland Race Course; a high-priced
Keeneland sales yearling

Anne M. Eberhardt photos

From top, Thoroughbred Park in downtown Lexington; the Kentucky Derby Museum; Cigar, one of racing's leading earners, at home at the Kentucky Horse Park

David Young; Anne M. Eberhardt

Clockwise from left, a horse and rider clear a fence at the Kentucky Rolex Three-Day Event; participants in the Junior League Horse Show; Standardbreds racing at The Red Mile

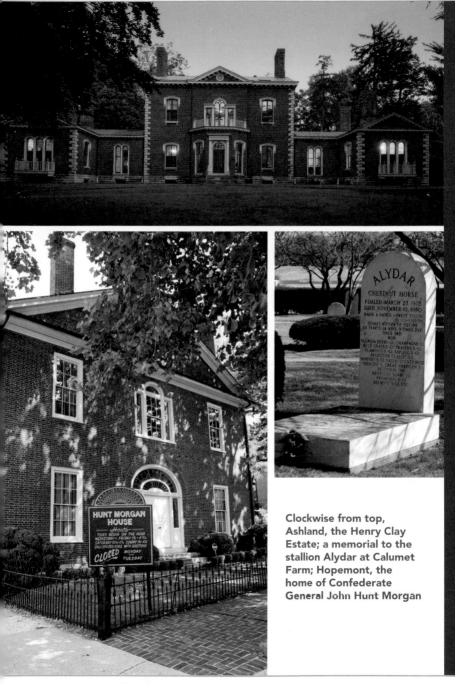

Clockwise from top, Ashland, the Henry Clay Estate; a memorial to the stallion Alydar at Calumet Farm; Hopemont, the home of Confederate General John Hunt Morgan

Above, the Lexington Cemetery is a national arboretum; inset, McConnell Springs, the site of Lexington's founding; below, Rupp Arena, where the UK Wildcat basketball team plays

From top, Buffalo
Trace Distillery;
the Kentucky
state capitol; the
Louisville Slugger
Museum

Clockwise from top, Mammoth Cave; Shaker Village at Pleasant Hill;
Natural Bridge; Abraham Lincoln's boyhood home

The difference is in the house's interior. Gone is the subdued palette of beiges, eggshell whites, and browns that dominated the former décor; they have been replaced by a wide spectrum of vivid colors, from burnt orange to teal to sunburst gold. The bold colors complement hand-blocked wallpaper and dizzying patterns representative of the high Victorian era.

While some visitors have expressed dismay at the kaleidoscopic mix of colors and patterns on every available surface, the décor is true to what the Rowans and their guests would have known. The dining room, in shades of royal blue and gold, with its wallpaper design of stylized palm trees, evokes Italy's Kingdom of the Two Sicilies where John Rowan Jr. served as the U.S. charge d'affaires in the late 1840s. An upstairs bedroom offers an unapologetic meshing of florals, stripes, and geometric prints. The best parlor boasts the most colorful décor: green and yellow wallpaper; a teal carpet with gold, red, and black accents; and wine red damask draperies.

Still, even with the dramatic flash of colors, visitors inevitably gravitate to the grand piano tucked into a niche beside the fireplace. Just the place for a young man, enamored of the gracious lifestyle, to compose a song that was to become synonymous with a state, a time in history, and a longing for home — a place where the sun will shine forever bright.

501 East Stephen Foster Ave. on U.S. Highway 150.
(502) 348-3502. www.parks.ky.gov.
Costumed hostesses offer guided tours of the house daily from 9:00 a.m.–5:00 p.m. Admission: $3.50–5.50. During the summer months, *Stephen Foster — The Musical*, is performed under the stars in the park's amphitheater.

THE ABBEY AT GETHSEMANI

The abbey, peacefully slumbering under an afternoon sun and surrounded by rolling green hills, evokes a scene straight from Provence or Tuscany. You can imagine hearing the carillon of bells summoning an order of cowled monks to evensong. But this isn't medieval France or Italy; it's 21st-century Kentucky.

In a rural setting just outside of Bardstown, the Abbey at Gethsemani looms large — both in structure and importance in the commonwealth's history. On a crisp October day in 1848 in Burgundy, France — the season when the vines were thick with grapes waiting to be harvested for the region's legendary wine — a group of 44 monks and laymen set out from the Abbey of Melleray to found a new monastery in an area known for its bourbon rather than its wine.

Upon closer study, the seemingly unusual choice proved to be not so unusual after all. For in a largely Protestant state, the area around Bardstown was often jokingly referred to as the "Catholic Holy Land," being the home parish of Father Stephen Badin, the first Catholic priest to be ordained in the United States.

Unlike the chain of missions established by the Jesuit and Franciscan orders in the Southwest, whose purpose was to convert and educate the Indians, Gethsemani's order of Trappist monks sought a contemplative, solitary life where scholarship, not salvation of souls, was their primary concern.

Experiencing the serenity of Gethsemani today, visitors might find it difficult to imagine that its early years were fraught with enough chaos and turbulence to test the faith of even the most devout. The stalwart monks suffered freezing winters and sweltering summers, the outbreak of the Civil War (during which they managed to maintain an uneasy neutrality), a decline in the number of new monks, and financial hardships.

Gethsemani's future was uncertain at best until the mid-20th century when two things occurred that aided in the Abbey's rebirth — the international fame of one of its monks and the success of one of its commercial endeavors.

Thomas Merton's years at Gethsemani began in 1941 and continued until his untimely accidental death by electrocution in 1968. During those years, Merton's writings, especially his autobiography, *The Seven Story Mountain*, acquainted millions of readers with the Trappist way of life, and a record number of visitors arrived at Gethsemani's gates to experience the idyllic existence of which Merton wrote. Merton's fame also spurred international attention, allowing Gethsemani to blossom into a recognized center for interreligious dialogue. In addition to being the country's oldest Trappist monastery, the Order's policy of tolerance also made the Abbey at Gethsemani the first Trappist monastery to allow female visitors, and it became one of the earliest to allow weekend retreats, not just for Catholics but for lay people of all faiths.

If Thomas Merton put the Abbey on the map, Gethsemani Farms has kept it there. What began as a local endeavor in a former cow barn has mushroomed into an international distribution of the monastery's acclaimed food products. From Bardstown to Berlin, people are familiar with the products made by Gethsemani's monks — bread, honey, Trappist cheese, fruitcakes, and fudge — the latter two liberally laced with the area's famed bourbon.

Today visitors come to walk the paths that Thomas Merton trod or to work alongside the monks currently in residence. Some seek religious dialogue; others seek silence. All are welcome as Thomas Merton said, "to entertain silence in the heart and listen for the voice of God, to pray for your own discovery."

3642 Monks Rd. (502) 549-3117. www.monks.org.
For farm orders, call (800) 549-0912.

WICKLAND

Wickland, a historic mansion on the outskirts of Bardstown, is known as the home of three governors, but only two of them — Charles Wickliffe and his grandson, J.C.W. Beckham — were governors of Kentucky. The third, Wickliffe's son Robert (they believed in keeping governorships all in the family), was governor of Louisiana in the years leading up to the Civil War.

The three-story mansion is regarded as one of the finest examples of Georgian-style architecture in the state. Self-guided tours of the house and grounds are available, and the Honorable Order of Kentucky Colonels hosts an annual barbecue on the grounds the day after the Kentucky Derby.

550 Bloomfield Rd. (502) 348-4877.

Other Attractions

OSCAR GETZ MUSEUM OF WHISKEY HISTORY AND BARDSTOWN HISTORICAL MUSEUM

This double museum occupies the main floor of historic Spalding Hall, which was built in 1826 and has variously been used as a seminary, Civil War hospital, orphanage, and prep school for boys.

The Oscar Getz Museum of Whiskey History traces the development of spirits from the tax-prompted Whiskey Rebellion of America's Colonial period (the 18th-century copper stills are a favorite with visitors) through the dry years of Prohibition (one exhibit shows how Kentuckians got around this by using whiskey for "medicinal purposes") up to today.

One of the most popular exhibits is a whimsical mural, "What's

Your Pleasure, Mr. President?" showing 43 U.S. presidents holding their favorite libations (Presidents Bill Clinton, George W. Bush, and Barack Obama haven't been added yet). From George Washington (Madeira, port, claret, and champagne) to George H.W. Bush (gin and tonic) our chief executives have been a cocktail-loving bunch, yet only one — Harry Truman — brought joy to the heart of Kentuckians. His choice: Bourbon and branch water.

The Bardstown Historical Museum features items covering 200 years of local history; it is an extremely eclectic collection, ranging from Indian relics and a replica of the first steamboat to papers from the pioneer period and Abraham Lincoln family documents.

114 North Fifth St. (502) 348-2999.
www.whiskeymuseum.com.
Tuesday–Saturday, 10:00 a.m.–4:00 p.m.;
Sunday, noon–4:00 p.m. (November through April) and
Monday–Friday, 10:00 a.m.–5:00 p.m.;
Saturday, 10:00 a.m.–4:00 p.m., and Sunday, noon–4:00 p.m.
(May through October).

KENTUCKY RAILWAY MUSEUM

One of the country's oldest rail museums began in the early 1950s with the donation of one Louisville & Nashville Railroad steam locomotive. Since then it has grown into an impressive display of more than 100 different cars and locomotives and a 3,000-square-foot model train building. The real crowd pleaser, however, is the 22-mile round trip between New Haven and Boston ("where else can you go between New Haven and Boston and still be in the same state?" the conductor will joke) through the Rolling Fork River Valley on a restored passenger train. Today's train enthusiasts will follow the same route that carried Union supplies during the Civil War, when trains were regularly attacked by Confederate General John Hunt Morgan and his raiders.

136 South Main St., New Haven.

(502) 549-5470. www.kyrail.org.

Monday–Saturday, 10:00 a.m.–4:00 p.m.; Sunday, noon–4:00 p.m.

Museum admission: adults, $5; children, $2.

BERNHEIM FOREST

This nature preserve's Arboretum Way loops around the 250-acre arboretum, created from a design by Frederick Law Olmstead, who also designed New York City's Central Park. Within these 250 acres are exotic species of trees, from the Tennessee pink redbud to the sweetbay magnolia, the full moon maple to the silky dogwood, the Carolina silverbell to the Japanese lilac. This is a place for peaceful contemplation, where the sigh of the breeze and the gentle ripples of Lake Nevin are the only sounds. Visitors fish in the lake, wander the paths and trails that wind through the forest for more than 35 miles, or meditate in the shade of a star magnolia or a double-flowered Higan cherry tree without skateboarders, boaters, or off-road vehicles to disturb the stillness.

Located in Clermont, just outside Bardstown, the forest was a gift to the people of Kentucky from Isaac Wolfe Bernheim, a German immigrant who settled in the commonwealth and rose from humble beginnings as an itinerant peddler to become a successful distiller, selling his bourbon under the I.W. Harper brand.

In addition to picnic areas and 16 miles of paved road for bicycling, Bernheim Forest offers interactive outdoor exhibits such as scent and sound mazes and a discovery walkabout, a canopy tree walk rising 75 feet off the forest floor, an artists-in-residence program, an award-winning visitors center built from recycled wood, and 6,000 species of trees, shrubs, native grasslands, natural woodlands, and a cypress-tupelo swamp scattered across 14,000 acres.

Bernheim Forest is off I-65 on State Highway 245 in Clermont, not far from the Jim Beam Distillery. (502) 955-8512. www.bernheim.org.
Open daily (except Christmas and New Year's Day) 7:00 a.m.– sunset. Admission is free Monday–Friday, although there is a donation box at the main gate. Weekend fees are $5 per passenger car.

MY OLD KENTUCKY DINNER TRAIN

If you're nostalgic about the golden era of train travel, here is an excursion you won't want to miss. My Old Kentucky Dinner Train, composed of three beautifully restored 1940s vintage railroad cars, takes passengers on a two-hour lunch or dinner excursion. The 40-mile round trip begins in Bardstown and travels through scenic Limestone Springs and the Bernheim Forest before returning to Bardstown. Historic note: One of the cars carried former President Dwight Eisenhower's family during his funeral procession and is reputed to be haunted.

602 North 3rd St., Bardstown. (502) 348-7300.
www.kydinnertrain.com. The train operates year-round on a
varied schedule. Lunch prices: adults, $59.95; children, $34.95.
Dinner prices: adults, $79.95; children, $44.95.

Hodgenville

ABRAHAM LINCOLN BIRTHPLACE NATIONAL HISTORIC SITE

Illinois and Indiana have also claimed the nation's 16th president, but his humble story began here in this town south of Bardstown. At the Abraham Lincoln Birthplace National Historical Site, thousands of people annually climb the 56 steps (one for each year in Lincoln's life) leading up to what at first seems to be a Greek or Roman temple, over the entrance to which is carved the phrase, "With malice toward none, with charity for all." The building's classical lines, columns, and solid marble façade are just a lovely shell for the real treasure that lies inside.

The crude one-room log cabin with a dirt floor and single window is not, as some think, the actual cabin where the future president was born on February 12, 1809, but a replica of the original, which stood here on what was once his father's Sinking Spring Farm. The cabin serves as a sobering reminder of how high Lincoln rose from these humble origins to the highest office in the land.

Many visitors comment on the resemblance of the exterior structure to the Lincoln Memorial in Washington, D.C. It is also worth noting that among those who helped to raise money for the site were Mark Twain, attorney William Jennings Bryan, and journalist Ida Tarbell. The cornerstone for the building was laid by President Theodore Roosevelt in 1909, and two years later the memorial was dedicated by another president, William Howard Taft.

2995 Lincoln Farm Rd., off US 31-E. (270) 358-3137.
www.nps.gov/abli. Labor Day–Memorial Day,
8:00 a.m.–4:45 p.m.; Memorial Day–Labor Day,
8:00 a.m.–6:45 p.m. Free admission.

ABRAHAM LINCOLN BOYHOOD HOME

Lincoln was two years old when his family moved to this farm on nearby Knob Creek (now part of the National Historic Site) in 1811. As he recalls in his autobiography, the farm was the first place he had any recollection of, and he spent the (somewhat) carefree early years working — helping his father build the split-rail fences of the type that now surround the log cabin (another replica) — and playing. (One anecdote has it that as a boy Lincoln fell into Knob Creek and was pulled to safety by a quick-thinking schoolmate who grabbed a tree branch and fished him out of the water.)

These were happy years for young Abe, and it was a sad day when at the age of seven — his family having lost the title to the property — he was forced to leave Kentucky behind for Indiana.

US 31E. (270) 358-3137. www.nps.gov/abli. Open daylight hours
year round. Free admission.

Springfield

LINCOLN HOMESTEAD STATE PARK

This historic site features a replica of the modest log cabin where Lincoln's father, Thomas, was raised, and of the blacksmith shop where he learned his trade. Another dwelling, Berry House, is the actual structure where Lincoln's mother, Nancy Hanks, was born and spent her life until Thomas proposed (some say in front of the house's large fireplace). Also part of the park (but located about a mile from the main entrance) is the home of Mordecai Lincoln, Abraham's favorite uncle. Built in 1797, the house is now listed on the National Register of Historic Places and is the only structure belonging to a Lincoln family member that still stands on its original site.

5079 Lincoln Park Rd. (859) 336-7461. www.parks.ky.gov.

The Kentucky Bourbon Trail ®

As you have learned, bourbon is America's only native spirit (so declared by an act of Congress), and 95 percent of that bourbon is produced in Kentucky. For the past couple of years, the Kentucky Distillers' Association, the Kentucky Department of Tourism, and the various Convention & Visitors Bureaus along the trail have been actively working to promote the Kentucky Bourbon Trail. For the purposes of this book, I have included the trail in this chapter because Bardstown, home to two distilleries and with two more on its outskirts, is officially known as the "Bourbon Capital of the World." However, please note that the trail can be picked up in Lexington, Frankfort, Louisville, or any of the towns with a distillery (see map on page 159).

If you begin the trail in Louisville, you might want to get in a bourbon state of mind over a Manhattan or an Old-Fashioned at the Maker's Mark Bourbon House & Lounge at the Fourth Street Live entertainment complex. While the eight distilleries aren't lined up side by side the way the wineries are in Napa Valley and require a bit more planning (and driving), the entire trail is easily doable

DID YOU KNOW

Every time you take a sip of good Kentucky bourbon, you have the Reverend Elijah Craig to thank. It was allegedly Craig who in the 18th century mixed corn, rye, and barley malt to come up with the spirit used in the common-wealth's signature beverage, the mint julep.

over a long weekend. As added incentive, the Kentucky Bourbon Trail has been named by *National Geographic Traveler* magazine as one of its "Drives of a Lifetime — the World's Greatest Scenic Routes." Impressive when you consider that its company includes some other pretty spectacular drives such as Italy's Amalfi Coast, the Hana Highway on Maui, and England's Cornish Coast.

DISTILLERIES

Buffalo Trace Distillery, 113 Great Buffalo Trace, Frankfort. (800) 654-8471. www.buffalotrace.com. Monday–Friday, 9:00 a.m.–3:00 p.m.; Saturday, 10:00 a.m.–2:00 p.m., with tours starting on the hour.

Just north of Frankfort, Buffalo Trace is in a picturesque setting of rolling hills, where the Kentucky River intersects the former historic trace, down which buffalo, Indians, and settlers all traveled. You'll definitely want to take the tour (which I think is the most informative of all the distillery tours) demonstrating the aging process of this highly acclaimed whiskey. Buffalo Trace is the oldest continuously operating distillery in the United States and the first distillery to market single barrel bourbon commercially.

Four Roses Distillery, 1224 Bonds Mill Rd., Lawrenceburg. (502) 839-3436, ext. 18. www.fourroses.us. Monday–Saturday, 9:00 a.m.–3:00 p.m., with tours starting on the hour.

Four Roses' Spanish mission-style architecture may seem out of place in the Bluegrass, but the lovely story of how the distillery got its name is sure to bring out the romantic in every visitor. It came about when the founder, enamored of a beautiful Southern belle, proposed marriage. She replied that if her answer was yes, she would wear a red rose corsage at a ball the following evening. Entering the ballroom and seeing the object of his affection wearing a corsage of four perfect red roses, the young man was inspired to name his bourbon Four Roses. Romantic legend aside, it's still the bourbon that gives Four Roses its *raison d'etre*.

Heaven Hill Distillery, 1311 Gilkey Run Rd., Bardstown. (502) 337-1000. www.heavenhill.com. Tuesday–Saturday, 10:00 a.m.– 5:00 p.m.; Sunday, 12 noon–4:00 p.m.

Heaven Hill is America's largest independent family-owned producer of distilled spirits, and the second-largest holder of aging bourbon whiskey in the United States, with an inventory exceeding 850,000 barrels. Since the repeal of Prohibition in the 1930s, Heaven Hill has filled more than 5½ million barrels of bourbon. Visitors can tour the impressive Bourbon Heritage Center and sample Heaven Hill's best in a barrel-shaped (what else?) tasting room.

Jim Beam Distillery, 526 Happy Hollow Rd., Clermont. (502) 543-9877. www.jimbeam.com. Monday–Saturday, 9:00 a.m.–4:30 p.m.; Sunday, 1:00–4:00 p.m.

Jim Beam's outpost at Clermont is set amidst a gorgeous backdrop of rolling hills in a tableau rivaling anything Napa or Sonoma has to offer. Jim Beam is the world's largest bourbon distiller, specializing in the production of handcrafted small batch bourbons, and producing what is consistently rated one of the two top-selling whiskies in the United States. Visitors can experience the rich history and heritage of Jim Beam by touring the T. Jeremiah Beam home where they can watch a video on the "First Family of Bourbon," followed by a tasting of the distillery's award-winning bourbons.

Maker's Mark Distillery, 3350 Burks Spring Rd., Loretto. (270) 865-2099. www.makersmark.com. Monday–Saturday, 10:30 a.m.–3:30 p.m., with tours on the half-hour. Tours are offered on Sunday at 1:30 p.m., 2:30 p.m., and 3:30 p.m. (March through December).

In the town of Loretto, south of Bardstown, Maker's Mark Distillery's distinctive red and black buildings make a lovely picture in a rustic setting on the banks of Hardin's Creek. Here, in the nation's oldest working bourbon distillery on its original site (since 1805), you can take a guided tour to discover why Maker's Mark crafts its bourbon in batches of fewer than 19 barrels and even hand dip your own bottle in its signature red wax. Then head to the state-of-the-art tasting room, which looks as if Phillipe Stark and Ian Schrager could have designed it. If you're hungry, there is also a gourmet sandwich shop, the Toll Gate Café.

Tom Moore Distillery, 300 Barton Rd., Bardstown. (502) 348-3774. www.1792bourbon.com. Tours: Monday–Friday, 9:30 a.m. and 1:30 p.m. Reservations required.

Called one of the "best kept secrets in Kentucky," Tom Moore Distillery — formerly the Barton Distillery — is the newest distillery to become part of the trail. Its super premium 1792 Ridgemont Reserve gets its name from the year Kentucky joined the Union.

Wild Turkey Distillery, 1525 Tyrone Rd., Lawrenceburg. (502) 839-4544. www.wildturkey.com. Tours: Monday–Saturday, 9:00 a.m., 10:30 a.m., 12:30 p.m., and 2:30 p.m.

Wild Turkey Distillery sits on the crest of a hill overlooking the Kentucky River. It originally opened in 1855 as a grocery store specializing in teas, coffees, and, of course, spirits. It didn't get its name, however, until 1940 when a distillery executive brought a private supply along to enjoy with friends on their annual wild turkey hunt. It proved so popular that the following year the group requested some of that "wild turkey" bourbon. Legendary Master Distiller Jimmy Russell is considered to be the elder statesman of the commonwealth's bourbon industry. One of Wild Turkey's unique features is the 40-foot-high column still.

Woodford Reserve Distillery, 7855 McCracken Pike, Versailles. (859) 879-1812. www.woodfordreserve.com. Tours: Tuesday–Saturday, 10:00 a.m.–3:00 p.m.; Sunday, 1:00 p.m., 2:00 p.m., and 3:00 p.m. (April through December).

The oldest and smallest distillery in Kentucky, Woodford Reserve is a National Historic Landmark, situated on Glenn's Creek among picturesque horse farms. With a distilling tradition dating back to Elijah Pepper in the early 1800s, Woodford now produces the official bourbon of the Kentucky Derby, Belmont Stakes, and England's Epsom Derby. On a tour, you can get a close-up look at the triple distillation process — from the copper pot still to the only surviving stone aging warehouses in America.

All distillery tours are free, except for Woodford Reserve which charges $5. At your first distillery stop, ask for your Bourbon Trail passport. Get it stamped after each tour, and if you collect stamps from all eight distilleries, you will be eligible for a commemorative T-shirt. For more information, visit www.kybourbontrail.com.

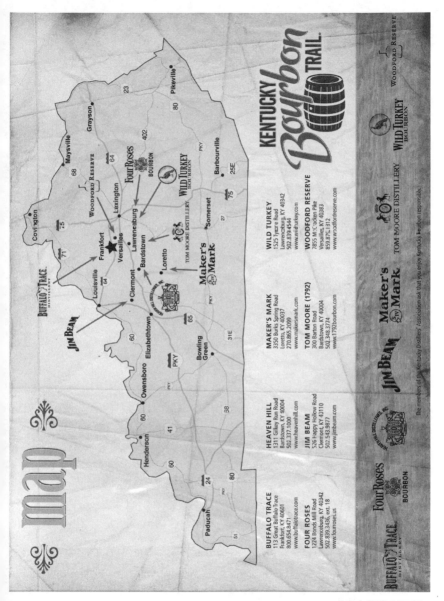

Kentucky Distillers' Association

KENTUCKY BOURBON TRAIL® MAP

10

A Bit Farther Afield

For the purposes of this book I have focused on the parts of the state at the epicenter of the horse industry — Lexington and its environs for the scope of the breeding and racing operations and Louisville as the site of the country's premier Thoroughbred race. The attractions these two areas alone offer are too numerous for any single visit.

Having said that, I can't neglect to mention several Kentucky places outside the Lexington/Louisville area that are so special they warrant a visit. If you have time, you should try to visit one (or all).

MAMMOTH CAVE NATIONAL PARK, CAVE CITY

The slender crystal columns suspended from the cave ceiling sparkle as if sprinkled with fairy dust. In the dim light, the eerie formations sprouting from the walls and rising from the floor cast shadows that are remarkably lifelike. It's easy to imagine you're in the company of ghosts when standing several hundred feet beneath the sandstone-capped ridges of Mammoth Cave National Park — the most extensive cave system on earth, with more than 350 miles of passageways mapped and surveyed.

Each year nearly two million visitors from all parts of the globe descend on Cave City in the west central part of the state to visit Mammoth Cave and marvel at its natural wonders — Roosevelt's

Dome, Giant's Coffin, Grand Central Station, Snowball Room, Bridal Altar, and Star Chamber — formations of stalactites, stalagmites, and columns, naturally carved from stone and eroded by water, their beauty frozen in time.

These travelers have been visiting since 1810, making Mammoth Cave the first major tourist attraction in the United States, pre-dating all other national parks and monuments. Among the notables who have descended into the Rotunda and risked neck strain to gaze in awe at the Fairy Ceiling are writers Charles Dickens and Ralph Waldo Emerson, actor Edwin Booth, opera singer Jenny Lind, naturalist John Muir, and Russian prince Alexis.

But the cave's exploration began well before the mid-1800s. Evidence indicates that as far back as 3000 B.C. Indians of the Archaic period entered Mammoth's recesses in search of minerals. Yet even after 5,000 years of intermittent exploration, much of Mammoth Cave remains shrouded in mystery and the full extent of this water-formed labyrinthine maze may never be known.

Today's explorers come not in search of minerals but of memories, and in this area Mammoth Cave (a National Park since 1941, a UNESCO World Heritage Site since 1981, and an International Biosphere Reserve since 1990) doesn't disappoint.

There are tours for beginners — the 30-minute, self-guided Cave Discovery Tour, which allows visitors a brief peek into the cave environment on a three-quarter mile loop — and tours for thrill-seekers — the six-and-a-half hour, five-and-a-half-mile Wild Cave Tour, where participants free climb cave walls and squeeze through passages only nine inches high in some places. There are even tours for expert cavers who, donning headlamps, crawl and climb through the cave on undeveloped trails.

Most visitors seem content to take the middle road on the two-hour Frozen Niagara Tour, which allows them the thrill of Mammoth Cave's most magnificent formations without having to shimmy through miniscule openings and wear unflattering headgear.

Regardless of the tour they choose, visitors will experience the world's most diverse cave ecosystem. It is home to many species so specialized they could not survive anywhere else — creatures such as the cave cricket, cave beetle, cave salamander, and the eyeless crayfish and shrimp, whose existence for millions of years in near total darkness has caused them no longer to need eyes.

Mammoth Cave's natural wonders and bio-diversity, however, are only part of its appeal. The cave area reeks of history. As a plaque in the park states, "the feet of woodland Indians, long hunters, slaves and old cave guides have passed this way," all sharing a common heritage — the hilly country, the Green and Nolin rivers (between whose scenic valleys the park nestles), and the great underground labyrinth that make Mammoth Cave National Park unique.

Two of the cave's most fascinating characters were Stephen Bishop and Dr. John Croghan. Bishop, an African-American slave, became one of the cave's most famous guides in the years prior to the Civil War and is credited with extensive mapping of its passageways. Croghan, a physician, bought Mammoth Cave Estate, which included the cave, in 1839 and set about establishing a "hospital" for tuberculosis patients 160 feet below ground, believing that vapors from the cave would provide a cure. His well-intentioned experiment proved a failure, and in a supreme twist of irony both Croghan and Bishop succumbed to tuberculosis.

The ghosts of Bishop and Croghan, along with many others, may well still inhabit Mammoth Cave. For in addition to the secrets of nature, other, darker secrets remain untold in the cave's shadowy corridors. Eerie tales of unexplained sounds, strange flickering lights, and disembodied footsteps abound. So do haunting legends such as the one about a young girl who, driven by her unrequited love for her handsome tutor, lured him to Echo River in the depths of the cave and abandoned him there. He was never seen again.

Then, of course, there's Floyd Collins, a caver whose tragic story became a media cause célèbre in 1925, when, during an attempt to discover another entrance into Mammoth Cave, he became trapped in Sand Cave where he remained for nearly two weeks. Despite numerous rescue attempts and relentless press coverage of his plight, he perished, appropriately enough, on a Friday the 13th.

The park has plenty to delight visitors above ground as well. The 52,830 acres of the park include more than 70 miles of hiking trails on the cave's north side and 27 miles of river on the Green and Nolin for boating, canoeing, and fishing. Bird lovers can see a wide variety of birds, both great — bald eagle — and small — ruby-throated hummingbird. Both the great and little blue heron thrive here, as do the sandhill crane and osprey.

This is a place of unparalleled beauty and grandeur, whose secrets have not been given up willingly — a place that has often exacted a high price from those who sought to conquer it.

The park is open year-round except for Christmas Day. Call (270) 758-2328 or (270) 758-2180 or go to www.nps.gov/maca for additional information. There are overnight accommodations in the park lodge, cottages, and at campsites.

NATIONAL CORVETTE MUSEUM, BOWLING GREEN

The vivid red and yellow structure visible from Interstate 65 in Bowling Green in the west central part of the state could be mistaken for a large yellow mushroom impaled on a red toothpick, or even a psychedelic spaceship come to roost. But the flamboyant architecture is only a warm-up for the flamboyant product on display inside.

If a generation of Americans fell in love with the country's lost highways and the freedom to explore them after reading Jack Kerouac's iconic book *On the Road*, they fell in love with the vehicle that would allow them to do so in style when the first Corvette rolled off the General Motors assembly line in 1953. If ever a car defined the romance and freedom of the open road, it was the Corvette.

The sporty little roadster, with its fish-like fins and rainbow-hued colors, was the 20th-century version of the elegant carriage, only with more horsepower. The Corvette was America's original sports car, the mechanized "King of the Road," and since its opening in 1994 the National Corvette Museum has been its palace. Within the museum's 68,000 square feet are more than 70 Corvette models — including one of the first off the assembly line (sticker price: a whopping — at that time — $3,498), and the historic one millionth 'Vette, the latter donated by Chevrolet, the car's manufacturer.

Located only a quarter of a mile from the assembly plant where all Corvettes have been manufactured since 1981, the museum is a monument to kinder, gentler times when you could fill up your tank for $5, and the back roads of America offered a "Huck Finn on wheels" kind of adventure. The Corvette as a motorized "charger" (white or otherwise) may always have been something of an urban myth, as financially out of reach for most motoring "knights" as a Mercedes or a Rolls is to today's driver, but as a myth it was a lot of fun. The museum, with its vast collection of Corvette-related photos, movies and videos, advertisements, and memorabilia, enhances both the mythology and the fun.

Full-scale dioramas show classic Corvette models in period

settings, one of the most popular being a scene from the 1960s TV series *Route 66*, in which two young road warriors, traveling America in their Corvette, got in and out of trouble in hamlets along the way. The *TV Guide* may have listed Martin Milner and George Maharis as the show's stars, but for most viewers, the snappy baby blue 'Vette was the real star.

Other popular exhibits include a 1983 Corvette — the only one left in existence — and the two-tone autumn colored 1981 'Vette with a dark-claret trim owned by the late country singer Marty Robbins, who was also an enthusiastic race car driver.

The Corvette's entire timeline is covered in the museum — from a film on the car's beginnings shown in the 200-seat theater to futuristic designs and concepts still in the embryonic stages.

Back to the Huck Finn comparison, if Huck were to stumble out of the pages of Twain's novel and get a gander at the treasures the National Corvette Museum holds, he would no doubt beg to trade his raft for a shiny new model.

350 Corvette Dr., Bowling Green, off I-65. (270) 781-7973. www.corvettemuseum.com. Open daily, except for Easter, Thanksgiving, Christmas Eve and Day, and New Year's Day, 8:00 a.m.–5:00 p.m. Admission: adults, $8; seniors, $6; children 6–16, $4.50; 5 and under, free.

LAND BETWEEN THE LAKES NATIONAL RECREATION AREA, SOUTHWESTERN KENTUCKY

If you are looking for impressive statistics, how about this? The second-largest inland peninsula in the United States (after Michigan's Upper Peninsula) and the second largest contiguous block of forested public land east of the Mississippi River. Some 170,000 acres of pristine land and 300 miles of undeveloped shoreline. Three sites on the National Register of Historic Places. The largest publicly owned bison herd east of the Mississippi River.

Where, one might ask, can you find such a treasure?

If you are like approximately two million other visitors a year, you can find it picturesquely sprawled across the borders of rural southwestern Kentucky and northwestern Tennessee. The Land Between the Lakes National Recreation Area, the 360-square-mile peninsula formed when the Cumberland and Tennessee Rivers were impounded to create Kentucky Lake and Lake Barkley, is a water sports enthusiast's paradise, offering swimming, boating, waterskiing, and some of the best fishing in the southeastern United States.

But the slender column of land running between the two lakes offers more than a water wonderland. Designated a National Recreation Area in 1963 by President John F. Kennedy, Land Between the Lakes also offers 200 miles of hiking, biking, and OHV trails, and 100 miles of horse trails (along with Wranglers' Campground where campers are invited to camp alongside their horses).

The Land Between the Lakes also focuses on history, wildlife conservation, and education. In the former category, LBL has three sites on the National Register of Historic Places, including Fort Henry, site of a major Civil War battle. It also has The Homeplace, an 1850s-era farm, where through a blend of artifacts, historic structures, and a re-creation of farm activities such as cultivating and harvesting tobacco and shearing sheep, visitors get a picture of 19th-century rural America.

When it comes to wildlife, LBL offers visitors their pick. They can look for deer, wild turkey, bobcat, osprey, and eagle. In the winter the area hosts an eagle population of 100, with 12 to 16 active nesting sites. At the Nature Station, located deep in the woods between Honker and Hematite lakes, animal lovers can see great horned owls, coyotes, and the reclusive red wolf (if they're lucky). But the most popular place to get up close and personal with the recreation area's animal population is the 750-acre Elk and Bison Prairie, a restoration of a native prairie habitat that once thrived in western Kentucky and upper Tennessee. Here, herds of elk and bison roam freely as they did two centuries ago.

For some education mixed in with your fun, take in a show at the Golden Pond Visitor Center's 81-seat theater and state-of-the-art planetarium. Here you can observe such phenomena as white dwarves, black holes, and life on Mars, unveiled across the planetarium's 40-foot dome.

At the end of the day, there are plenty of places to kick back and relax. The Kentucky Department of Parks operates three resort parks on the borders of LBL: Lake Barkley State Resort Park, Kenlake State Resort Park, and Kentucky Dam Village State Resort Park.

100 Van Morgan Dr., Golden Pond. (270) 924-2000 or (800) LBL-7077. www.lbl.org.

RED RIVER GORGE AND NATURAL BRIDGE STATE RESORT PARK, EASTERN KENTUCKY

It is rare for any state to have a spot as beautiful and untamed as the Red River Gorge Geological Area, but to have another, Natural Bridge State Resort Park, adjacent is a double bonus.

The Red River Gorge Geological Area, designated a National Natural Landmark, is located in the Daniel Boone National Forest, about an hour-and-a-half drive from Lexington. One of the most scenic areas in the state, it encompasses 29,000 acres of cliffs, rock shelters, caves, waterfalls, and mountain pools as well as some 100 natural arches, the largest concentration east of the Rocky Mountains. These beautiful arches, tortured into unique formations by millions of years of wind and water, are awe-inspiring, especially in the fall when they are softened by the brilliant colors of the forest.

Probably the best known (and most accessible) of the Gorge's many attractions is Sky Bridge, from which you get an excellent view of the Clifty Wilderness. The section of the Red River that runs through the Clifty is the only river in Kentucky to be designated a National Wild and Scenic River.

The Gorge has hundreds of miles of official and unofficial hiking trails, ranging from easy (Angel Windows, Whistling Arch, and Chimney Top) to moderate (Double Arch, Silver Mine Arch) to rugged and extremely difficult (Sheltowee Trace, Raven's Rock). These trails can provide enjoyment, whether you opt for a day hike or a backpacking trip into the interior. However, extreme caution should be taken as many of the trails parallel the rim of high cliffs and bluffs. The Gorge is also a paradise for rock climbers, although a certain level of expertise is necessary; it is not a destination for beginners.

About 10 miles from the entrance to the Gorge is the entrance to Natural Bridge State Resort Park, one of the state's most popular vacation destinations. If the flaming colors of fall best show off the Gorge's spectacular beauty, spring is the season that best showcases Natural Bridge, with some 100 species of wildflowers blanketing the woods and trails.

Natural Bridge was one of the commonwealth's original state parks, dating back to the late 19th century when a track built by the Kentucky Union Railway to ship lumber did double duty for a sightseeing train carrying those eager to see the dramatic landscape.

Of course, the park's main attraction is the sandstone formation from which it gets its name — accessible by a sky lift or a hiking trail, the three-quarter-mile Original Trail that begins at the park lodge and ends at the bridge. At 65 feet high and 78 feet long, Natural Bridge is the largest of the park's arches, taking nearly 65 million years to be carved by the raging waters of the Red River.

Other hiking trails worth checking out are the three-quarter-mile Battleship Rock Climb (note the word climb), the Laurel Ridge Trail (with carved rock staircases and deep drops through the Devil's Gulch and Needle Eye), and the Sand Gap Trail (at seven-and-a-half miles the park's most challenging).

Hiking may be the most popular activity, but it is far from the only one. Kids love the river theme of the giant swimming pool — with its water jets and floor bubblers — tucked between 15-acre Hoedown Island and the cliff behind Hemlock Lodge, the park's beautiful main accommodation.

Adult anglers find a paradise here, with bass, bream, crappie, catfish, and rainbow trout in the 54-acre Mill Creek Lake, and environmentalists will delight in the fact that nearly half of the park's 2,500 acres is set aside as a nature preserve.

2135 Natural Bridge Rd., Slade.
www.parks.ky.gov
For reservations at Hemlock Lodge, call (800) 325-1710, or to reserve a campsite, go to www.reserveamerica.com.
The Red River Gorge covers three counties (Powell, Menifee, and Wolfe). Take Slade exit (#33) and turn left at the bottom of the exit to Hwy. 15. Turning either right or left will take you into the Gorge. (606) 663-2852. www.redrivergorge.org.

CUMBERLAND GAP NATIONAL HISTORICAL PARK, SOUTHEASTERN KENTUCKY

If the Cumberland Gap had a literary equivalent, it would be the looking glass in *Alice in Wonderland*, through which the heroine caught a glimpse of a parallel world. The Gap, on the borders of Kentucky, Virginia, and Tennessee, provided a similar function for early day settlers — a passageway through the seemingly impenetrable wall of the Allegheny Mountains, and a chance to cross the dividing line from the familiar East into the unknown West.

The first known white man to negotiate the Gap successfully was Dr. Thomas Walker, who came through here in April 1750 (see Chapter 1). Daniel Boone followed in 1775, and over the next 30 years some 12,000 pioneers poured through the 800-foot natural "break" in the Cumberland Mountains.

Pioneers of a different sort — tourists — are still pouring through, visiting the 20,000-acre Cumberland Gap National Historical Park, just south of Middlesboro off Highway 25E. Some of the scenery here is nearly as pristine and unspoiled as it was two-and-a-half centuries ago, and the views from nearly everywhere in the park are stunning. Among the best: 2,440-foot Pinnacle Overlook, from the top of which you can see three states, and White Rock, where on a clear day you can see all the way to the Great Smoky Mountains on the border of Tennessee and North Carolina. The two scenic overlooks are connected by a hiking trail, the Ridge Trail, which runs the entire length of the park. (There are 70 miles of hiking trails that wind through native eastern forest, and range in length from one-quarter mile to 21 miles.)

Other popular spots include the Sand Cave, situated next to a waterfall that tumbles 100 feet from top to bottom and Goose Neck Sink, a huge sinkhole, allegedly the result of a collapsed cave.

Hensley Settlement, atop Brush Mountain, has been preserved to showcase what life was like for two Appalachian families who moved to the mountain in the early 20th century to escape "civilization." They created their own version of Walden Pond that continued until 1951, when Sherman Hensley, the founder, also became the last of the family to leave the mountain.

Another must-see is Cumberland Crafts. Located in the park's visitor center, it offers handicrafts typical of southern Appalachia.

<hr/>

The Visitor Center is located on U.S Hwy. 25E just south of Middlesboro. Open daily (except Christmas Day) 8:00 a.m.–5:00 p.m.
(606) 248-2817. www.nps.gov/cuga.
Note: The four-mile Skyland Drive up to Pinnacle Overlook may sometimes be closed due to adverse weather conditions.

CUMBERLAND FALLS STATE RESORT PARK, CORBIN

There are only two places in the world where a rare phenomenon — the moonbow, which occurs regularly during cycles of the full moon — can be found: At Victoria Falls in Africa and here, at Cumberland Falls in southeastern Kentucky. The falls attract about a half million visitors a year, making this one of the two most visited sites in the state (the other being Natural Bridge). With a width of 125 feet and a drop of 68 feet, Cumberland Falls might be a miniature version of Victoria — which spans two countries, Zambia and Zimbabwe — but try telling that to the throngs of visitors who line the upper and lower observation areas for a look at the lacy spirals of water spilling into the boulder-studded river below.

A perpetual mist surrounds the falls, and this, in part, is what causes the moonbow. The scientific explanation is the light of the full moon is reflected and refracted in the delicate droplets of the mist, causing the arc to appear a ghostly white rather than multihued. Maybe, but it's poetry and not science that I think of when I see the moonbow.

Cumberland Falls State Resort Park, located just southwest of Corbin, in the middle of the Daniel Boone National Forest, has plenty to complement its main attraction. For starters, there are 20 miles of hiking trails. A good mix of easy, moderate, and difficult, the trails take visitors to scenic vistas throughout the park, and one — the 10.5-mile Moonbow Trail — is a segment of the Sheltowee Trace, which extends the entire length of the national forest.

Fishing, swimming, and horseback riding are also available, and a professional outfitter, five miles east of the resort, can get you geared up for canoeing, kayaking, and rafting on the Cumberland, designated as one of Kentucky's wild rivers.

Dupont Lodge has 51 rooms, a number of one- and two-bedroom cottages scattered throughout the forest, 50 campsites with electricity and water hookups, and a dining room with spectacular views of the forest all the way down to the river.

7351 Ky. 90, Corbin. (606) 528-4121. www.parks.ky.gov.
For reservations at Dupont Lodge, call (800) 325-0063.

Note: If you want to see a moonbow, the phenomenon only occurs during full moons. The park has a schedule of dates every year for when full moons will occur.

BIG SOUTH FORK RECREATIONAL AREA, STEARNS

Less than a half-hour drive from the entrance of Cumberland Falls State Resort Park is another of Kentucky's scenic wonders — the 125,000-acre Big South Fork Recreational Area, which covers parts of southeastern Kentucky and northeastern Tennessee. This is a place of contrasts — a checkerboard of opposites — jagged gorges and scarred fissures next to deep expanses of cool, green forest. The contrasts are so stark that it has an otherworldly feel.

In common with many of the state's other natural areas, Big South Fork offers plenty of opportunities to see Mother Nature's handiwork up close and personal on hiking trails (some 150 miles of trails that offer everything from one-mile loops to multi-day hikes), but most visitors come for an excursion on its Scenic Railway. The 100-year-old train, a relic of the Kentucky & Tennessee Railway, takes passengers on a 16-mile roundtrip journey that descends 600 feet into the gorge of the Big South Fork of the Cumberland River.

From the open-air train car, you get a close look at dense vegetation, through which you can glimpse flowing mountain streams and vertigo-inducing vistas. The trip takes you back to a time when coal and lumber camps sprang up in this part of Appalachia like mushrooms after a rainstorm. One of them, Blue Heron Coal Mining Camp, is a Southern cousin of the Old West ghost town. Built by the Stearns Coal and Lumber Company in 1937 for its employees, it was all but abandoned by the early 1950s. The recreated camp allows visitors to take in oral history exhibits (you can actually hear recorded voices of miners talking about the hardships they endured), walk into the entrance of a coal mine, and cross the river on a coal tipple bridge.

Another former mining camp, Barthell, has overnight accommodations in the former miners' quarters, although the cabins are a considerable upgrade from what the miners got when they were built around the turn of the last century. (For reservations, call (888) 550-5748; rates fluctuate according to season, but begin at about $100 per night.)

Big South Fork National Recreation Area is in Stearns in McCreary County and continues south across the Tennessee state line. To get there, take I-75 south to Highway 92 and then west to Stearns. There is an alternate route on Highway 700, intersecting US 27 near Whitley City. If you choose the latter route, you can see Kentucky's highest waterfall (Yahoo Falls, which drops 113 feet). You might be disappointed if you are expecting a Niagara-like rush of water; Yahoo Falls is just a thin trickle at best; if the weather is dry, it all but vanishes. www.nps.gov/biso. Visitor information: (423) 286-7275.

100 Henderson St. (800) 462-5664.
www.bsfsry.com. Trains run every Wednesday, Thursday, and
Friday at 11:00 a.m.; Saturday at 11:00 a.m.
and 2:30 p.m.; and Sunday at 2:30 p.m., April–October.
Trains run Thursday–Saturday at 1:00 p.m., November–December.
Rates are $18 for adults, $16.50 for seniors, and $9 for children.

BREAKS INTERSTATE PARK, SOUTHEASTERN KENTUCKY

A gray curtain of early morning mist descends on the rugged gorge known as "the Grand Canyon of the South." You might not be able to see it, but you can definitely hear it: the thundering rush of water struggling to escape the confines of the canyon. This is a place of mystery, harboring many ghosts — of prehistoric animals and ancient Indian tribes, of long-ago lovers who vanished into its recesses, of those who have done murder and those who have had murder done.

It's easy to let your imagination run wild at Breaks Interstate Park, which straddles the Kentucky and Virginia state line between Elkhorn City, Kentucky, and Haysi, Virginia, and is one of only two interstate parks in the nation. Jointly administered by a commission of individuals from both states, Breaks' 4,500 heavily forested acres attract nearly a million visitors annually. They come to fish in the serene pools, hike 12 miles of meandering trails, raft the Class V-VI rapids of the Russell Fork River, and marvel at the beauty of the lavender blooms of the Catawba rhododendron in spring, and the russets, golds, and burnt oranges of the foliage in the fall.

For most visitors, the park's centerpiece is the five-mile-long, 1,600-foot deep canyon formed more than 250 million years ago by the raging waters of the Russell Fork, a tributary of the Big Sandy River, on their headlong dash to meet up with the Ohio River. The "breaks" in Pine Mountain made by the water resulted in the sandstone gorge, the largest and deepest east of the Mississippi River. Its majesty can best be appreciated from four scenic overlooks throughout the park.

Visual splendor aside, Breaks Interstate Park has plenty to offer. Unique rock formations, a honeycomb of caves, and wildlife, including the majestic golden eagle, add to the park's allure, as does its colorful history.

That history, combined with legend and lore, features a fascinating cast of characters. While Daniel Boone is credited with discovering the Breaks on several attempts to forge a trail into Kentucky, in the end the challenging terrain proved too much for him and his companions.

Boone is only one of the figures associated with Breaks. Shawnee Indians used the Pow Wow Cave for secret ceremonies, and Englishman John Swift is said to have buried a fortune in silver here. The Hatfields and McCoys warred across the state line, while on a more peaceful note the literary "Trail of the Lonesome Pines" wends its way around the park.

Visitors will find plenty to keep them occupied. A rustic lodge built on the rim of the canyon, cottages nestled in the woods, and a campground offering more than 120 campsites provide accommodations, while recreational opportunities include an Olympic-sized swimming pool, horseback riding, hiking, mountain biking, picnic shelters, and an amphitheater deep in the woods, where every Labor Day weekend some 10,000 people gather for the Tri-County Gospel Sing.

Every October when the Army Corps of Engineers releases water into the Russell Fork River, whitewater rafting, kayaking, and canoeing enthusiasts come from all over the world to test their skill and their mettle. If you have any doubts about the park's claim to some of the best whitewater in the South, just consider some of the rapids' names: 20 Stitches, Broken Nose, and Triple Drop.

You may have to demonstrate your whitewater credentials — or at least your bravado — to get a spot on a raft, but all you need is a love of natural beauty and the spirit of adventure that characterized this region's early pioneers to appreciate Kentucky's and Virginia's shared jewel.

Breaks Interstate Park is located seven miles from Elkhorn City, Ky. and eight miles from Haysi, Va. (800) 982-5122. www.breakspark.com.

NEWPORT AQUARIUM, NEWPORT

"If there is magic on this planet, it is contained in water ... its substance reaches everywhere, it touches the past and present and prepares the future."

Those words from scientist Loren Eisely, etched on a wall plaque at the Newport Aquarium, the anchor attraction at Northern Kentucky entertainment complex Newport on the Levee, provide a fitting send-off for visitors beginning their journey through this Ohio River landmark. A million gallons of water showcase thousands of animals from around the world in 65 different exhibits covering 121,000 square feet of space.

This is an animal nirvana for species such as the King and Gentoo penguins whose Antarctic-like Kingdom of Penguins exhibit, with its falling snow and icy waters, makes the perfect backdrop for their comical antics. The penguins, which always seem to be playing to their delighted audiences, may be the most popular residents at the aquarium, but other species have their fan clubs as well.

The collection of Native American alligators that laze on the banks of a recreated Louisiana bayou lures curious onlookers who have never seen the scaly creatures up close. Visitors to the Indonesian rainforest exhibit may purchase a cup of nectar to attract free-flying scarlet lorikeets before moving on to giggle over the antics of Asian small-clawed otters — frolicking like a litter of puppies — in their simulated river, or gasp in mock horror at the size of the jewel-toned Burmese pythons.

At Shark Central, a replication of a field biology station, nervous children (and adults) are encouraged to conquer their fear and reach out and touch the swimming sharks circling around them. Closer to home, there is even a diorama of an Ohio riverbank, complete with gar, lake sturgeon, and bass.

Rated one of the top aquariums in the country by *Zagat Travel Guide*, Newport Aquarium's stunning exhibits range from Dangerous and Deadly, where poisonous predators such as dart frogs and piranhas lurk in wait for their unsuspecting prey, to the less-intimidating Jellyfish Gallery where diaphanous, fragile jellyfish, including the unusual moon jelly, float in a watery ballet. In the Amazon Flooded Forest, visitors meander along the lower level of an Amazon Rainforest, peering at freshwater stingrays and pacu, a South American freshwater fish that is a close relative of the piranha, while the Coral Reef display takes them through a glass tunnel for an up-close look at one of the planet's most colorful and fragile ecosystems.

In the Duke Energy Theater, visitors can enjoy a spectacular view of the aquarium's 385,000-gallon shark tank, but if that isn't close enough, in the Surrounded by Sharks exhibit only two-and-a-half inches of acrylic separates them from several species of sharks, stingrays, and sea turtles. This exhibit is also home to Sweet Pea, a female shark ray who has become something of a cause célèbre in aquarium circles. The Newport Aquarium made history by becoming the first aquarium in the Western Hemisphere to display a manta shark, and then again made headlines when it introduced a male shark ray to Sweet Pea, initiating the world's first dedicated Shark Ray breeding program.

Throughout the aquarium, visitors can marvel at the exotica, collected from all seven continents, while learning such fascinating "fun facts" as:

* A shark can lose more than 30,000 teeth in a lifetime (it just keeps replacing them).

* Blue tangs are yellow when they are born.

* Sea turtles can roam over a thousand miles of ocean in a year's time.

* The gender of a turtle is determined by temperature — cooler temperatures produce males, while warmer ones produce females.

* Every six seconds the earth loses a swath of rainforest equivalent in size to a football field.

**One Aquarium Way. (800) 406-3474.
www.newportaquarium.com. Open 365 days a year, with
scheduled hours of operation varying depending on season.
Admission: adults, $18; children, $11.**

Kentucky Festivals

Kentuckians love a good party and throughout the year find the time to celebrate everything from mountain laurels (Louisville) and dogwoods (Hopkinsville) to blues (Henderson) and bluegrass (Rosine) music. They honor esteemed sons (Daniel Boone, Winchester) and daughters (Rosemary Clooney, Maysville), and for some reason not understood, Raggedy Ann (Cynthiana) and Ronald McDonald (Versailles).

They pay tribute to apples (Paintsville), sorghum (Springfield), chickens (London), mushrooms (Irvine), gourds (Taylorsville), pumpkins (Paris), and country ham (Lebanon). They celebrate gold (Fort Knox) and gingerbread (Hindman), fiddlers (Renfro Valley) and fossils (Clarksville).

It's the horse … the horse, of course, but it's also the llama and alpaca (Georgetown), and even the buffalo (Stamping Ground).

While it would be impossible to detail all the festivities (a complete list of events can be gotten from the Kentucky Department of Tourism), a few deserve special recognition:

APRIL

Kentucky Derby Festival, Louisville. Festival organizers like to say they have stretched two minutes (the Derby race) into two weeks (the festival, the commonwealth's largest single annual event, is held the third weekend in April through Derby Day, always the first Saturday in May).

It kicks off with "Thunder Over Louisville," the nation's largest annual fireworks extravaganza, and concludes with crowd favorites, the Pegasus Parade and the Great Steamboat Race on the Ohio River. In between is a slate of eclectic events ranging from balloon races to bed races. One of the quirkiest activities is the Run for the

Rosé, where restaurant employees navigate a downtown obstacle course bearing trays of glasses filled with grape juice.

Whether it's open-to-the-public street dances and concerts or celebrity-laden private balls, this is one festival that has something for everyone.

∞∞∞∞∞∞

(502) 584-6383. www.kdf.org.

MAY

International Bar-B-Que Festival, Owensboro. Every southern state lives and dies by its barbecue tradition and Kentucky is no exception. Owensboro is considered the commonwealth's barbecue central, and every second weekend in May, cooking teams compete to see who comes away with the title of Barbecue King or Queen.

Fierce competition and fiercer aromas (sizzling chicken, bubbling burgoo, redolent ribs) rule the day as local cooking teams vie for the Governor's Cup, using jealously guarded secret recipes that even the CIA would be hard put to infiltrate.

Barbecue may be the star attraction, but there is a large supporting cast: carnival rides, pie and mutton-eating contests, a horseshoe tournament, classic car show, and non-stop entertainment.

∞∞∞∞∞∞

Downtown. (800) 489-1131. www.bbqfest.com.

JUNE

Great American Brass Band Festival, Danville. This is one to warm the cockles of the hearts of John Philip Sousa, Professor Harold Hill, and anyone else who loves the pomp and circumstance of world-class brass bands. Hosted by Danville's own hometown band, the Advocate Brass Band, the festival provides four days of wholesome family fun. From parades to picnics, petting zoos to pancake breakfasts, and, of course, plenty of free concerts, it has all the appeal of a lazy summer day in a Norman Rockwell canvas. America should have more festivals like this one.

(606) 236-4692. www.gabbf.com.

SEPTEMBER

Kentucky Bourbon Festival, Bardstown. The town designated "America's Bourbon Capital" celebrates its most famous product every September with a series of activities ranging from seminars (want to learn about the ancient craft of barrel making?) to tastings (the perennially popular cooking with bourbon). There is an art exhibit and a golf tournament, a bourbon breakfast, and a bartenders' challenge. You can even rub tuxedoed elbows with master distillers at a black-tie Bourbon Gala. The dates for the festival vary, but it runs from Thursday until Saturday mid-month.

(800) 638-4877. www.kybourbonfestival.com.

11

Where to Stay

Part of any trip is finding the right place to stay, whether it be a historic inn with a resident ghost, a hip boutique hotel with its own art gallery, a bed-and-breakfast that overlooks a horse farm, a resort property on a former horse farm, or even a castle. You can find them all in the Central Kentucky area.

Kentucky's Historic Inns

What do a former girls' academy, a one-time jail, and an old Shaker meeting house have in common? For a traveler to the commonwealth, they are all places to spend the night and at the same time sample a piece of Kentucky's rich history.

The stately white-columned mansion nestled beneath equally stately magnolia trees in a pastoral setting in Harrodsburg may have began in 1845 as a school for privileged young ladies, but today the **Beaumont Inn** is one of Kentucky's most celebrated inns. Operating first as the Greenville Institute, then the Daughters College, and finally Beaumont College, the facility was converted to an inn in 1919, and today the antebellum Beaumont Inn has 31 guest rooms in three buildings — the Main Inn, Greystone House, and Goddard Hall. A fourth, Bell Cottage, once used for accommodations, now houses the spa.

A bastion of Southern civility, the inn's décor features antiques-filled rooms, hallways lined with portraits of Confederate generals, and a parlor where guests congregate around the Steinway piano for a pre-dinner sherry. (If they prefer Kentucky bourbon to sherry, their meeting spot is the Old Owl Tavern or the recently opened Owl's Nest adjacent to the main building.) Regardless of where they meet for pre-prandial libations, all converge on the inn's dining room for dishes such as the Kentucky cured country ham, yellow-legged fried chicken, corn pudding, and cornmeal batter cakes.

It's a short drive from the Beaumont Inn to **Shaker Village of Pleasant Hill**, but it's light years removed from a former boarding school for pampered young ladies to a communal dwelling place for a religious sect that espoused simple living. Among the rolling hills along the palisades of the Kentucky River, this National Historic Landmark offers visitors the option of staying in one of 73 rooms in 13 restored 19th-century buildings scattered throughout the village. All accommodations are furnished with finely crafted reproduction Shaker furniture and hand-woven rugs and curtains.

The candlelit Trustees' Office Dining Room has costumed wait staff serving bountiful family-style meals featuring homemade breads, a Shaker dish of the day, and mouth-watering desserts such as lemon or chess pie.

Iron bars on the windows, 30-inch thick stone walls, and a heavy steel door slamming shut behind you may not sound like a typical tourist accommodation, but at Bardstown's **Jailer's Inn**, guests can "do time" in style.

If you have your doubts, just check out the circa 1819 inn's six guest rooms. Okay, you can still slumber on one of two original bunks in the black and white jail cell (the only room still resembling a cell, it is popular with the younger members of the family), but the remaining accommodations are not likely to provoke a riot, lavishly appointed as they are in a variety of styles. Choose from among the antiques-filled Victorian Room or the Art Deco-inspired Library Room or the summery feel of the Garden Room's wicker and floral prints. It is equally difficult to imagine — over hot coffee and breakfast in the charming courtyard — that this same courtyard served as the gallows for the most unfortunate prisoners during the 200-year period when the building served as the Nelson County Jail.

Old Talbott Tavern, just down the street from the Jailer's Inn, is arguably Kentucky's most famous inn. In operation since the late 1700s, it has the distinction of being the oldest coaching inn west of the Alleghenies, and has played host to just about every hero and scoundrel who passed through Kentucky on his way to somewhere else. Exiled French King Louis Phillipe stayed here with his entourage and painted murals on the upstairs walls. Less artistic are the bullet holes in the now-faded paintings, courtesy of another guest, outlaw Jesse James.

Today, five individually decorated rooms are all named after a famous (or infamous) visitor. They include the Lincoln Room, named in honor of the 16th president who was born 20 miles away in Hodgenville and came here with his parents; the General's Room, named for two distinguished generals who slept here more than a century apart — George Rogers Clark and George S. Patton; and the Daniel Boone Room, honoring the famed frontiersman who overnighted here while giving a deposition in a land dispute.

Boone would no doubt be honored to discover that he rated a room named for him at the Talbott Tavern, but he would be positively thrilled to find that he had an entire hotel bearing his name in Berea. **Boone Tavern,** situated on the old Dixie Highway in the town's College Square, has been in continuous operation since its opening in 1909. Run by Berea College, the tavern's 58 guest rooms feature reproduction Early American furniture handcrafted from cherry, oak, and pine by students at the college.

Other students in period costume serve in the dining room where visitors delight in such traditional southern fare as chicken flakes in a bird's nest (a rich, creamy concoction served in a nest of crispy potatoes) and the Tavern's signature spoonbread, a dish that has inspired an annual three-day festival every fall.

Thanks to a recent multi-million-dollar renovation, Boone Tavern is so newly sparkling that if old Dan'l were to show up today in buckskins and muddy moccasins, he would probably be shown the door.

Begun in 1780 and completed in 1821, what is now **Doe Run Inn** has seen its share of history. Its site, south of Louisville, on Doe Run Creek, was discovered in 1778 by Squire Boone, brother of Daniel, and records show that Thomas Lincoln, father of Abe, worked here as a stonemason on the newer part of the building. It was used as a mill until 1901 when it opened as a family resort with the somewhat unpleasant name of Sulphur Wells Hotel. In the 1950s the name was changed to Doe Run Inn, the idea presumably being that baby deer held more appeal than something associated with a chemistry lab. The inn has 11 rooms as well as accommodations in surrounding cabins, and an onsite restaurant with home-style cooking, including country ham with red-eye gravy and hush puppies, salad dressings made from scratch, and green beans, which, according to the owner, "are cooked all day."

So whether you want to live the simple life, go to a fancy finishing school, or land in jail, Kentucky's historic inns offer you the opportunity.

Beaumont Inn, 638 Beaumont Inn Dr., Harrodsburg. (800) 352-3992. www.beaumontinn.com. Rates range from $95 to $205.

Shaker Village of Pleasant Hill, 3501 Lexington Rd. (US 68),
Harrodsburg. (800) 734-5611. www.shakervillageky.org.
Rates from $75 to $225.

Jailer's Inn, 111 West Stephen Foster Ave., Bardstown.
(800) 948-5551. www.jailersinn.com. Rates from $80 to $215.

Old Talbott Tavern, 107 West Stephen Foster Ave.,
Bardstown. (800) 482-8376. www.talbotts.com.
Rates from $65 to $109.

Boone Tavern, 100 Main St. N, Berea. (800) 366-9358.
www.boonetavernhotel.com. Rates from $130 to $150.

Doe Run Inn, 500 Doe Run Hotel Rd., Bradenburg.
(270) 422-2982. www.doeruninn.com. Rates from $45 to $77.

Staying in Cinderella's Castle

CASTLE POST HOTEL

The turreted stone castle looks as if it could have been transported from England's Camelot to Kentucky's Bluegrass and that it's just waiting for a tournament of knights carrying their ladies' banners, but Castle Post is the newest addition to the area's hospitality scene. Not quite a hotel (although it does have 16 rooms) and not quite a B & B (although it does include breakfast), a stay at Castle Post is much like a stay at the home of a good friend — if that friend happens to be royalty.

The exterior is quite impressive enough, but the interior is opulent, with lots of dark wood paneling, gilded mirrors, chandeliers, decorative molding, ceiling frescoes, and a spectacular sweeping staircase just made for the descent of a king or queen. Public rooms include a library, music room, drawing room, dining room, and an enormous ballroom.

230 Pisgah Pike, Woodford County. (859) 879-1000.
www.thecastlepost.com. Rates in the Castle's main building range
from $375 to $600; rates for the four turret rooms are
$1,150 per night (all include breakfast and a three-course dinner).

And now, for something a bit more conventional …

Lexington

THE CROWNE PLAZA CAMPBELL HOUSE

Featured on the TV Travel Channel's *Great Escape*s and in *Southern Living* magazine, this imposing white-columned hotel with the appearance of an over-sized antebellum mansion has always been popular with the horse set. It has been said that more Thoroughbred deals have been done in the hotel's restaurant than anywhere else in town. The Campbell House is particularly abuzz in October when both Keeneland's fall racing meet and the University of Kentucky football season are in full swing. The hotel underwent a total renovation in 2007.

1375 South Broadway. (859) 255-4281.
www.thecampbellhouse.net. Rates begin at $140.

THE GRATZ PARK INN

Located in one of Lexington's most historic neighborhoods, this 41-room inn (of which six are suites) provides a peaceful retreat for discriminating travelers. Each room is individually decorated with antique reproduction furniture, including four-poster beds in many rooms and paintings showcasing regional artists.

After a day at the races or touring the city's sights, there's no better place to relax over a premier Kentucky bourbon than the cozy bar of Jonathan's Restaurant (see Chapter 12). With dark wood paneling and a fireplace, the bar resembles an English gentlemen's club.

If you are of the notion that a ghost only enhances a hotel experience, this is the spot for you. There are tales of a mischievous specter roaming the corridors, presumably a holdover from the building's early days as Lexington's morgue. The Gratz Park Inn is listed on the National Register of Historic Places.

120 West Second St. (859) 231-1777. www.gratzparkinn.com. Rates from $179 to $425. The inn is pet friendly, but requires a non-refundable $100 pet fee.

HYATT REGENCY LEXINGTON

This newly renovated 365-room property has arguably the best location in Lexington. Located next door to Rupp Arena where the University of Kentucky plays basketball and within the same complex as the Shops at Lexington Center, it overlooks beautiful Triangle Park and is across the street from Victorian Square shopping and entertainment complex. With all that going for it, the only thing lacking is an appealing exterior design.

401 West High St., (859) 253-1234. www.lexington.hyatt.com. Rates from $119 to $209.

MARRIOTT GRIFFIN GATE RESORT

Lexington's only full-scale resort property, it is located four miles from downtown on the grounds of a former horse farm. The imposing entrance, beautifully landscaped with seasonal flowers and plants, leads up to The Mansion, formerly the restaurant and now a special-events venue. The resort features 409 guest rooms, including a seventh-floor presidential suite, an 18-hole Rees Jones-designed golf course, and a luxurious full-service spa. Two of the spa's most intriguing offerings are uniquely Kentucky — the mint julep body polish (no bourbon was harmed in the creation of this service) and the Bluegrass wrap, which utilizes local herbs.

1800 Newtown Pike. (859) 231-5100. www.marriott.com.
Rates begin at $179.

THE EMBASSY SUITES

Just across from the Marriott Griffin Gate Resort, the Embassy Suites, in its beautiful pastoral setting next to the University of Kentucky's Coldstream Research Farm, is very popular with the horse crowd.

1801 Newtown Pike. (859) 455-5000.
www.embassysuites1.hilton.com.
Rates from $119 to $209.

Louisville

21C MUSEUM HOTEL

There are immediate clues that this is not going to be your typical hotel. It might be the red plastic penguins gazing down from the building's roof like more benevolent versions of Edgar Allan Poe's ravens. It might be the chandelier swaying tipsily from a lamppost outside the hotel restaurant. It might be the eyes winking back at you from a mirror over a bathroom sink or the letters of the alphabet raining down the wall near a bank of elevators.

These are just a few of the more than 5,000 pieces of contemporary art that make up the collection of Steve Wilson and Laura Lee Brown, who opened 21C (for 21st century) in 2006 in five rehabbed buildings that once served as whiskey warehouses (many of the original features, such as exposed brick work, arches, and leaded glass transoms, remain).

It is the first hotel in the country devoted to exhibiting the work of living 21st-century artists. That work is displayed throughout the hotel — in guest rooms, in the Proof on Main restaurant (see Chapter 12), and in 9,000 square feet of exhibition space just off the lobby and continuing down a spiral ramp to a lower-level gallery.

The 90 guest rooms don't come equipped just with art but with 42-inch HDTV flat screen televisions and iPods as well as carefully thought out amenities such as custom-made bourbon and silver mint julep cups to enjoy it in.

⬦⬦⬦⬦⬦⬦⬦⬦⬦⬦

700 West Main St. (502) 217-6300. www.21cmuseumhotel.com. Rates from $209 to $359.

THE CAMBERLEY BROWN HOTEL (SEE CHAPTER 7)

THE GALT HOUSE HOTEL & SUITES

The largest hotel in Kentucky describes itself as Louisville's waterfront hotel, and with its location right on the Ohio River that is no exaggeration. The Galt House is composed of two towers — the Suite Tower and the RiVue (for Riverview) Tower. Linking the two is a glass conservatory that spans Fourth Street and is the site of Al J's Lounge with its unique 30-foot bar which doubles as a tropical fish tank. The new Rivue Restaurant is located on the rooftop and offers stunning views of the River City. Perhaps the hotel's most unique feature is the "Gallop for Glory." Modeled after Hollywood's Walk of Stars, it honors Kentucky Derby-winning jockeys with their handprints and signatures in cement.

**140 North Fourth St. (502) 589-5200. www.galthouse.com.
Rates from $119.**

THE SEELBACH HOTEL (SEE CHAPTER 7)

Bed and Breakfast Inns

Danville

THE GOLDEN LION BED & BREAKFAST

This is the place to stay if you want to keep up with the Joneses — literally. Innkeepers Jerry and Nancy Jones have studied the genealogy of the surname and if you are a Jones, they will be happy to assist you in your own genealogy. Each of the three suites is named after a prominent Jones — Cadwallader Jones, a 17th-century governor of the Bahamas; Nicholas Jones, a Revolutionary War patriot; and Griffin Jones, an 18th-century Virginia tobacco grower. Even if your last name isn't Jones, you will be welcome at this 1840 Greek Revival Mansion listed on the National Register of Historic Places.

**243 North Third St., (859) 583-1895. www.thegoldenlionbb.com.
Rates from $89 to $95.**

BRYAN HOUSE BED & BREAKFAST

A restored 1891 Queen Anne-style home known as the "jewel of Georgetown." Its three large suites all have antique period furnishings, and the inn is known for its lavish breakfasts featuring such mouth-watering dishes as Amaretto-stuffed waffles with raspberry maple syrup and eggs Napoleon on a roasted red pepper sauce.

**401 West Main St. (877) 296-3051.
www.bryanhousebnb.com. Rates from $99 to $165.**

Lexington

LYNDON HOUSE

Located in Lexington's historic district several blocks from downtown, Lyndon House looks like a typical Southern mansion on the outside but is unexpectedly quirky inside. The check-in desk is a replica of an English pub (a legendary symbol of hospitality, notes the owner) and the five rooms run the spectrum from saintly (the Shaker Suite whose furnishings reflect the simplicity of the Shaker life) to sinful (the Belle Brezing Room, named after Lexington's notorious madam). The house also has lovely gardens.

**507 North Broadway. (859) 420-2683. www.lyndonhouse.com.
Rates from $159 to $269.**

SWANN'S NEST AT CYGNET FARM

Nestled in rolling countryside less than a mile from Keeneland Race Course is Cygnet Farm, whose main house is now a lavishly appointed B & B. There are three rooms in the main house and two private suites in the house's guest quarters. Guests have use of the screened porch and courtyard overlooking a koi pond in warm weather and of the den with its cozy fireplace in the cooler months. The inn does not take children under age 16.

3463 Rosalie La. (859) 226-0095.

www.swannsnest.com.

Rates from $149 to $235.

Louisville

Louisville has the largest collections of Victorian homes in the United States. Many of these beautiful homes, located in the "Old Louisville" area have been turned into bed-and-breakfast establishments. This is but a small sampling of them.

CENTRAL PARK BED AND BREAKFAST

Built in 1884 and located just across the street from its namesake park, this B & B is listed on the National Register of Historic Places. The house has 18 rooms and nearly as many fireplaces (11). The seven guest rooms are all furnished with period furnishings and feature such elegant touches as oak woodwork, hammered brass fixtures, and stained glass.

1353 South Fourth St. (502) 638-1505. www.centralparkbandb.com.

Rates from $125 for the main inn to $175

for the Carriage House.

DUPONT MANSION

This Old Louisville gem is a rare example of Italianate-style architecture and features ornate carvings, plaster moldings, Italian marble fireplace, crystal chandeliers, 14-foot ceilings, and formal gardens. All eight rooms have fireplaces and each room is named for a famous person. Former partners in their railroad venture, Alfred I. Dupont and J.P. Morgan, would no doubt have been amused to learn that each has a suite named for him. Morgan would probably not be amused to learn that the room named for him is the least expensive ($129) while Dupont's is the most expensive ($239).

1317 South Fourth St. (502) 638-0045.
www.dupontmansion.com.

SAMUEL CULBERTSON MANSION

Pamper yourself with the opulence of the Gilded Age in this elegant Georgian mansion, said to be the most historic of Louisville's homes. When Samuel Culbertson built his 50-room mansion toward the end of the 19th century, it was considered the grandest on Louisville's "Millionaire's Row." Culbertson, a former president of Churchill Downs, cemented his place in track history when he came up with the idea of draping the Kentucky Derby winner with a garland of red roses in the shape of a horseshoe (for trivia buffs, the first winner to be so festooned was Burgoo in 1932). Today's visitor can get a taste of Culbertson's luxe lifestyle with an overnight stay in one of the mansion's seven rooms.

1432 South Third St. (502) 634-3100.
www.culbertsonmansion.com. Rates from $109 to $179.

1888 HISTORIC ROCKING HORSE MANOR

This Victorian mansion is Romanesque, a style even more rarely seen in Kentucky than Italianate, and features pocket doors, stained glass, and hand-carved fireplace mantels. The individually decorated rooms have lovely names such as Chelsea's Garden, Louise's Country Cottage, and the Irish Rose Room, or you can opt for the three-room eye-popping Grand Victorian Suite.

1022 South Third St. (502) 583-0408. www.rockinghorse-bb.com. Rates from $105 to $195 (excluding Derby week).

1853 INN AT WOODHAVEN

Although not located in Old Louisville, the inn nevertheless is gloriously situated. Set in its own lovely gardens, it is also in close proximity to Brown Park and Beargrass Nature Preserve, only a block away. Accommodations consist of four suites, three carriagehouse rooms, and the Rose Cottage. Guests can choose to enjoy their three-course breakfast in the dining room or in the privacy of their own room — a rarity in B & Bs.

401 South Hubbards La. (888) 895-1011. www.innatwoodhaven.com. Rates from $95 to $195.

Versailles

1823 HISTORIC ROSE HILL INN

This historic mansion, which from the outside looks like a gingerbread house with its gabled roof and ornate trim, offers seven impeccably decorated guest rooms, as well as a parlor, library, large front porch, and three acres of grounds. The 1823 Historic Rose Hill Inn has been voted "Best Bed and Breakfast in Kentucky" by readers of *Kentucky Monthly* magazine two years in a row.

233 Rose Hill Ave. (859) 873-5957. www.rosehillinn.com. Rates from $129 to $184.

MONTGOMERY INN

A restored 1911 Victorian inn, it has 10 individually decorated suites and offers such amenities as Egyptian cotton towels, Jacuzzi spa tubs, concierge services, and something that most bed and breakfasts don't — dinner! (Reservations necessary even for guests.) Relax on the old-fashioned wraparound porch or recline in the double hammock.

270 Montgomery Ave. (859) 251-4103. www.montgomeryinnbnb.com. Rates from $119 to $179.

STORYBOOK INN

Built circa 1843, this antebellum mansion offers the ultimate in Southern hospitality. No detail has been overlooked — from the high thread count sheets to the bountiful breakfasts. As for the rooms, the innkeepers are obviously film buffs as witness the names of the three suites: My Fair Lady, Casablanca, and Gone With the Wind. If you want more privacy, there is also the Huntsman's Chase Cottage, with two bedrooms and private deck.

277 Rose Hill Ave. (859) 879-9993. www.storybook-inn.com. Rates from $189 to $319.

12

Where to Eat

The art of Southern cooking is at its best in Kentucky. There's burgoo (a meaty stew) and Benedictine (a cucumber and cream cheese spread that is a staple on every Derby table), spoon bread and smoked barbecue, and, of course, finger-lickin' good fried chicken.

You already know that the Hot Brown, a hearty open-face sandwich, originated at Louisville's Brown Hotel and calls for bread, turkey, bacon, and pimentos browned under a broiler and then covered with Mornay sauce. You may not know that curing ham, Kentucky style, began in frontier times out of a necessity to preserve meat year-round. Country hams can be baked, simmered, or fried, with a multitude of recipes for each method, and all sorts of flavors — from fruit juice to cola to sweet pickle juice — can be simmered into the ham. For the ultimate Southern breakfast, Kentuckians like a fried country ham, sliced from the middle, paired with red-eye gravy, scrambled eggs, grits, and homemade beaten biscuits.

Every southern state from North Carolina to Tennessee to Texas trumpets the superiority of its barbecue, and Kentucky is no exception. While the commonwealth's barbecue central is in the western part of the state near Owensboro, you can find good barbecue — usually pork or mutton — statewide.

If Kentucky is famous for country ham and barbecue, it is positively legendary for fried chicken. Colonel Harland Sanders, the epitome of the Southern gentleman in his white suit and string tie, is a familiar face on five continents. His secret recipe, perfected in 1932 at a small roadside restaurant in Corbin in southeastern Kentucky, was the catalyst for today's international industry.

Though many Kentucky restaurants specialize in traditional Kentucky cooking, the state also has a number of cutting-edge restaurants whose chefs regularly appear in the pages of the top food magazines (particularly in Louisville and Lexington). Here's a tasty sampling of the best the area has to offer.

Bardstown

KURTZ RESTAURANT

The *New York Times* said this "was the place to go for definitive Southern fried chicken," and while I'm not one to take the *Times'* advice on definitive southern fried anything, in this case I have to agree. Ditto for the vegetables that accompany it and the homemade cobblers and pies and biscuit puddings for dessert. Oh, and don't forget the skillet-fried cornbread. Located just across from My Old Kentucky Home State Park, Kurtz's has been family owned and operated since 1937.

418 East Stephen Foster Ave. (502) 348-8964.
www.kurtz@bardstownparkview.com. Lunch: Tuesday–Saturday,
11:00 a.m.–3:00 p.m. Dinner: Tuesday–Saturday, 4:00–8:30 p.m.;
Sunday, noon–7:30 p.m.

Frankfort

RICK'S WHITE LIGHT DINER

If I didn't know better, I'd think Rick was in the witness protection program. What else could explain a CIA-trained chef hiding out in a hole-in-the-wall with menus plastered on the exterior, just across from Frankfort's "Singing" Bridge? Some stuffy restaurant's loss is Frankfort's gain as Rick does Memphis-style pulled pork barbecue, Louisiana Cajun dishes, and Kentucky bourbon pie — not to mention his signature "White Lightning" burgers — that will have you begging for more.

114 Bridge St. (502) 330-4262. Monday–Saturday, 8:00 a.m.–5:00 p.m.

SERAFINI'S

From its name you might expect this to be an Italian restaurant, and while they do have a few pasta dishes, the menu, for lack of a better description, is "just good old American food." One dish they are known for — not surprising considering the proximity to the Executive Mansion — is the Governor's Hot Brown.

243 West Broadway. (502) 875-5599. Lunch: Monday–Friday, 11:00 a.m.–3:00 p.m.; Saturday, noon–3:00 p.m. Dinner: Monday–Saturday, 4:30 p.m.–10:00 p.m.

Lexington

A LA LUCIE

Don't let the whimsical décor — faux zebra banquettes and tasseled red lamps that look as if they belong in a bordello — fool you. A la lucie's is serious about food. From the fried oyster stack to the grilled bourbon Tabasco pork chops, and oh yes, the lobster corn dog with hot Asian mustard dipping sauce, owner Lucie Meyers serves Lexington's most inventive food.

159 North Limestone. (859) 252-5277. www.alalucie.com.
Monday–Thursday, 4:00 p.m.–10:00 p.m.;
Friday and Saturday, 4:00 p.m.–11:00 p.m.

ALFALFA

This favorite with the college crowd when it was on the UK campus has lost none of its devotees since moving downtown. Don't be put off by the hippie-ish ambiance and heavy emphasis on vegetarian dishes; they'll happily feed carnivores as well.

141 East Main St. (859) 253-0014. www.alfalfarestaurant.com.
Monday & Tuesday, 8:00 a.m.–2:00 p.m.;
Wednesday & Thursday, 8:00 a.m.–9:00 p.m.;
Friday, 8:00 a.m.–2:00 p.m. and 5:30–10:00 p.m.;
Saturday, 9:00 a.m.–2:00 p.m. and 5:30–10:00 p.m. ;
Sunday, 9:00 a.m.–2:00 p.m.

ATOMIC CAFÉ

A little bit of the Caribbean in Lexington, with its wall murals, funky décor, tropical courtyard, tiki lights, reggae music, and drinks with paper umbrellas. The food, however, is anything but a cliché. Try the jerk chicken, conch fritters, and Cuban pork.

265 North Limestone. (859) 254-1969. www.atomiccafeky.com.
Tuesday, Wednesday, and Thursday, 4:00 p.m.–1:00 a.m.;
Friday & Saturday, 4:00 p.m.–2:30 a.m.

AZUR

Cool, stylish restaurant south of downtown. Colors are bold blues and greens and three sets of French doors lead from the inside to the shady brick patio, a favorite during the warm months. The cuisine is as inventive as the décor, with a heavy emphasis on Kentucky produce.

3070 Lakecrest Cir. in Beaumont Center. (859) 296-1007.
www.azurrestaurant.com.
Lunch: Monday–Saturday, 11:00 a.m.–3:00 p.m.
Dinner: nightly, 5:00–10:30 p.m.

BELLINI'S

This is one of the city's most glamorous restaurants, with an ornate bar that looks like it came straight from a movie set. Owned by two lifelong friends, both the children of immigrant families, Bellini's is Lexington's version of a typical trattoria and the place to satisfy your craving for *real* Italian fare.

115 West Main St. (859) 388-9583. www.bellinis.us. Lunch:
Monday–Friday, 11:30 a.m.–2:30 p.m. Dinner: Sunday–Thursday,
5:00–10:00 p.m.; Friday & Saturday, 5:00–11:00 p.m.

BUDDY'S BAR & GRILL

Named for a beloved cocker spaniel, it is the ultimate comfort food spot, whether you're in the mood for one of the daily omelet specials, fish and chips, a vegetable plate, or the double Buddy burger.

854 East High St. in Chevy Chase Village. (859) 335-1283.
www.buddysbarandgrill.com. Lunch: daily, 11:30 a.m.–5:00 p.m.
Dinner: Monday–Thursday, 5:00–10:00 p.m.;
Friday–Saturday, 5:00–11:00 p.m.

CHEAPSIDE BAR & GRILL

The second-level patio bar (named Lexington's best by a local magazine) is what you notice first. With its faux palm trees festooned with lights and splashy colors, it looks like a psychedelic dream from the '60s that you never woke up from. The extensive menu, however, has all the usual choices — burgers, salads, wraps, and what they call "the social grazing items" — a shrimp bowl, giant stuffed pretzel, and white veggie pizza among others — that are meant to be shared. This place is always lively, especially when UK students are in town.

131 Cheapside. (859) 254-0046. www.cheapsidebarandgrill.com.
Lunch: Monday–Friday, 11:30 a.m.–2:30 p.m.
Dinner: Monday–Saturday, 5:00 p.m.–12 midnight;
Sunday, 4:00 to 9:00 p.m. Brunch: Saturday & Sunday,
11:00 a.m.–4:00 p.m.

DUDLEY'S ON SHORT

At press time, this perennially popular restaurant is moving from its original location in a converted schoolhouse to a historic 1889 building in the heart of downtown Lexington's entertainment district. The new location features a first floor bar, dining room, and sidewalk café as well as a rooftop garden. The sophisticated menu, which includes such dishes as sautéed prawn and green garlic, goat cheese and beet torte, classic tournedos topped with crab meat, and Szechwan pepper-crusted tuna with port wine miso, will stay much the same, with a few additions such as gourmet pizzas and a tapas menu in the bar.

259 West Short St. (859) 252-1010. www.dudleysrestaurant.com.
Lunch: Monday–Saturday, 11:30 a.m.–2:30 p.m. Dinner:
Sunday–Thursday, 5:30–10:00 p.m.; Friday & Saturday,
5:30–11:00 p.m. Sunday brunch from 11:30 a.m.–2:30 p.m.

FLAG FORK HERB FARM

A quaint Lexington landmark that combines the Garden Café and a shop *Southern Living* magazine calls "one of the 200 best places to shop in the South." Located in the 1810 brick Thomas January cottage, it positively reeks of genteel ambiance. Diners in the café nosh on homemade soups, salads, quiches, and desserts as well as homemade beer cheese and sandwich choices including chicken salad, olive nut, and Benedictine and bacon, while overlooking a quarter-acre walled garden which features a butterfly garden.

900 North Broadway. (859) 252-6837. Open for lunch only
Wednesday–Saturday, 11:00 a.m.–2:00 p.m.
Reservations essential.

FURLONG'S

The owners are from Louisiana so specialties here are straight from the bayou. They offer Cajun dishes such as blackened frog legs over jambalaya, soft-shelled crabs, shrimp Creole, and shrimp and crawfish etoufée as well as more traditional fare.

735 East Main St. (859) 266-9000. www.furlongs.com.
Monday–Thursday, 4:00–10:00 p.m.; Friday & Saturday, 4:00–
11:00 p.m., Sunday brunch, 11:00 a.m.–3:00 p.m.

HANNA'S ON LIME

The slogan for this popular breakfast and lunch spot is "comfort food in a comfortable place." You may begin to doubt the "comfortable place" part when you try to find parking (there is none), but about the "comfort food" there can be no doubt. For breakfast there are pancakes, omelets, country ham, and biscuits, and for lunch, dishes your mother made, but maybe not as well as Hanna — meatloaf, chicken pot pie, salmon croquettes, fried chicken, and country fried steak. Hanna herself, a former basketball player for the Lady Wildcats, is as comfortable as her restaurant, so go ahead and circle the block a few times until you can find a parking place on the street or in a nearby lot. It's worth it.

214 South Limestone. (859) 252-6264. www.hannasonlime.com.
Breakfast: 7:00 a.m.–11:00 a.m. daily.
Lunch: 11:00 a.m.–2:00 p.m. daily.

JONATHAN'S AT GRATZ PARK INN

Chef Jonathan Lundy may look like a college frat boy, but his cooking has earned accolades from publications such as *Southern Living* and *Conde Nast Traveler*, and from a regular clientele who pack the restaurant at lunch just for his white cheddar pimento cheese or his deviled egg trio — eggs with smoked salmon, chive-asparagus, and country ham. Dinner suggestions include cracker-fried oysters over Tabasco maque choux, sea scallop hot brown, and grilled lamb chops with mint julep jelly. You can dine in the more formal dining room, on the patio in summer, or in my favorite — the clubby bar.

120 West Second St. in the Gratz Park Inn.
(859) 252-4949. www.jagp.info.
Lunch: Monday–Saturday, 11:00 a.m.–2:00 p.m.
Dinner: Monday–Saturday, 5:30 p.m.–10:00 p.m.
Sunday brunch, 11:00 a.m.–2:00 p.m.
Reservations suggested.

LE DEAUVILLE

Lexington's only true French bistro. If you need proof, just check out the menu: escargots de Bourgogne, charcuterie platter, duck confit with Lyonnaise potatoes, mussels served the French way (with thick pommes frites dipped in mayonnaise), and an assortment of French cheeses. Very popular with locals who pack the adjoining bar and sip wine at tables scattered across the sidewalk outside.

199 North Limestone. (859) 246-0999.
www.kygallery.com/Deauville/.
Dinner: Monday–Saturday, 5:30–11:00 p.m.

MALONE'S

Recognized as one of "America's top 10 steakhouses," Malone's has three Lexington locations that offer the finest in USDA prime beef along with fresh vegetables, luscious desserts, and a *Wine Spectator* award-winning wine list.

3347 Tates Creek Rd. in the Landsdowne Shoppes.
(859) 335-6500; 1920 Pleasant Ridge Dr. in Hamburg Pavilion.
(859) 264-8023; and 3735 Palomar Centre Dr. in Palomar Center.
(859) 977-2620. www.malonesrestaurant.com.
Open daily 11:15 a.m.–11:15 p.m.

THE MERRICK INN

A country inn feel in a tree-shaded urban setting, the Merrick Inn offers attentive service and a menu which describes itself as "signature Southern." Some of the dishes include almond chicken and pecan-crusted pork tenderloin and the fried banana peppers, a Lexington tradition. Dine inside or on the beautiful, flower-filled patio.

1074 Merrick Dr. off Tates Creek Rd. (859) 269-5417.
www.murrays-merrick.com. Monday–Thursday,
11:00 a.m.–10:00 p.m.; Friday, 11:00 a.m.–10:30 p.m.

METROPOL

Possibly my favorite Lexington restaurant is this one located in a skinny white cottage which served as the city's first post office. There's a miniscule bar downstairs and two smallish dining rooms upstairs. Some patrons complain about the cramped quarters, but I like to think of it as cozy in the way European bistros are. The food here is excellent with dishes such as scallops with mango chutney, a cassoulet that is as good as any they serve in France, and a poached shrimp appetizer that resembles shrimp cocktail, only the shrimp are warm.

307 West Short St. (859) 381-9493. www.metropolfinedining.com.
Dinner: Tuesday–Saturday, 5:30 p.m.–closing.

MURRAY'S

Owned by the same family as the Merrick Inn, this elegant spot is also in a converted mansion south of town. Once you drive up the circular driveway and see the imposing house and its garden (a popular spot for cocktails and outdoor dining), you suspect you're in for a treat. You're assured of it if you order the Kentucky bourbon ale-battered onion rings, chicken Marsala, or the baby back pork ribs with spicy apricot barbecue sauce.

3955 Harrodsburg Rd. (859) 219-9922. www.murrays-merrick.com.
Monday–Thursday, 11:00 a.m.–10:00 p.m.;
Friday, 11:00 a.m.–10:30 p.m.

PORTOFINO

Chic setting in a converted downtown warehouse with exposed walls, high-beamed ceilings, artwork, and a patio for summer dining. Excellent Italian fare, from the crispy fried ravioli with Angus beef and goat cheese to a variety of pastas and main dishes such as tenderloin cognac and lavender chicken.

249 East Main St. (859) 253-9300. www.portofinolexington.com.
Lunch: Monday–Friday, 11:00 a.m.–2:30 p.m.
Dinner: Sunday–Thursday, 5:00–10:00 p.m.; Friday & Saturday,
5:00–11:00 p.m.

ROSSI'S

This stylish bistro looks like it could be in New York City except for the New Orleans-style patio that is a favorite during warmer months. The long bar is also a favorite place for patrons to sip cocktails and nosh on an appetizer that may be the best in the city — bleu cheese chips, thin potato slices fried and sprinkled with bleu cheese crumbles, bacon, and scallions. But I warn you — after these, you may be too full for the Bourbon-glazed shrimp and sea scallops or the salmon seared over an open flame and topped with hollandaise or the herb-crusted prime rib, and that would be a shame.

1060 Chinoe Rd. in the Chinoe Centre.

(859) 335-8788. www.rossis-restaurant.com.

Dinner: Monday–Thursday,

5:00–10:00 p.m.; Friday & Saturday, 5:00–10:30 p.m.

Sunday brunch and Dinner: 11:00 a.m.–10:00 p.m.

Louisville

ASIATIQUE

Chef Peng Looi has brought the Pacific Rim to Louisville with such inventive and flavor-packed dishes as soft shell crab, roasted garlic tempura, crispy spinach, spicy miso aioli, and sweet chili basil and jam; Indochine-inspired grilled angus beef satay, and Maggi soy sauce and five-spice duck breast with pickled root vegetables and tomato lemongrass sambal. His five-course degustation menus are a bargain at $45.

1767 Bardstown Rd. (502) 451-2749.

www.asiatiquerestaurant.com.

Dinner: Monday–Thursday, 5:00–10:30 p.m.;

Friday & Saturday, 5:00–11:00 p.m. and Sunday, 4:30–10:00 p.m.

BAXTER STATION BAR & GRILL

The restaurant began in a century-old neighborhood tavern and in 1989 moved to its current location in historic Irish Hill (in tribute to the tavern, they still have 24 beers on tap). With "comfort food" from salmon croquettes to red beans and rice to a 7-ounce burger grilled to order, the Baxter Station Bar & Grill has been called one of "Louisville's 20 best" by the *Courier-Journal* newspaper.

1201 Payne St. (502) 584-1635. www.baxterstation.com.
Tuesday–Thursday, 11:30 a.m.–10:00 p.m.;
Friday, 11:30 a.m.–11:00 p.m. and Saturday, 4:30–11:00 p.m.

BOURBONS BISTRO

This is the place to go if you are seriously in need of a bourbon fix as they have more than 130 bourbons. The building, which dates back to 1877, is even more aged than their finest Pappy Van Winkle or Four Roses single barrel. With all the talk about the bourbon and the history, let's not forget the food. When I was there, I started off with fried cornmeal oysters served with a lemon horseradish aioli and peppered tomato banana sauce and moved on to the pan-seared pepper crusted ahi tuna with a peanut chili sauce. I really wanted dessert but was too full, so I settled for another bourbon.

2255 Frankfort Ave. (502) 894-8838. www.bourbonsbistro.com.
Dinner: Sunday–Thursday, 5:00–10:00 p.m. and Friday and Saturday,
5:00–11:00 p.m. Happy hour every day, 4:30–7:00 p.m.
(They have to do something with all that bourbon.)

BRISTOL BAR & GRILLE

A Louisville fixture since 1977 when it first opened on Bardstown Road, it has expanded to five locations in the metropolitan area. A typical meal might have you start off with the green chili won tons with guacamole, then go for the charbroiled New York strip steak with Henry Bain sauce, and finish up with lemon cheesecake with sour cream.

For all five locations and hours of operation, visit their Web site at www.bristolbarandgrille.com.

BUCK'S AT THE MAYFLOWER

An elegant restaurant amidst the splendor of Old Louisville mansions. Dishes such as bourbon pecan chicken stuffed with brie, beef tenderloin boursin, and pork chop calvados prove that the food is as elegant as the surroundings.

425 West Ormsby. (502) 637-5284. www.bucksrestaurantandbar.com. Dinner: Monday–Thursday, 5:00–10:00 p.m.; Friday & Saturday, 5:00–11:00 p.m. Reservations requested.

CAPTAIN'S QUARTERS RIVERSIDE GRILLE

Situated on a knoll overlooking the Ohio River where it meets Harrod's Creek, this is the place to go in nice weather for riverside dining. In the early 1800s the site was known as Harrod's Tavern, catering to thirsty rivermen; today, it is a vast dining and entertainment complex, seating 550 in the lodge, deck, and terrace areas. As you might imagine, the menu is heavily focused on all manner of seafood — from peel and eat shrimp and combination platters to more innovative fare such as low country shrimp and grits basted with Jack Daniels barbecue sauce. On weekends, there is live music on the patio.

◇◇◇◇◇◇◇◇◇◇◇◇

5700 Captain's Quarters Rd. (502) 228-1651. www.cqriverside.com. Monday–Thursday, 11:30 a.m.–10:00 p.m., Friday & Saturday, 11:30 a.m.–11:00 p.m., and Sunday, 10:30 a.m.–10:00 p.m.

CORBETT'S

A spot that espouses the virtues of local produce (Kentucky Bibb lettuce, for example). The menu is extensive, but if you're really hungry you can indulge in the seven-course grand tasting menu (for both vegetarians and non-vegetarians). If you are a vegetarian, you might get a dish such as sun-dried tomato fettuccine, asparagus, pine nuts, and feta cheese; a non-vegetarian might get scallops with Parmesan grits, asparagus, country ham, lobster, and herb butter.

◇◇◇◇◇◇◇◇◇◇◇◇

5050 Norton Healthcare Blvd. (502) 327-5058. www.corbettsrestaurant.com. Lunch: Monday–Friday, 11:00 a.m.–2:00 p.m. Dinner: Monday–Thursday and Sunday, 6:00–10:00 p.m.; Friday & Saturday, 6:00–11:00 p.m.

THE ENGLISH GRILL

The fine dining restaurant at the Brown Hotel, it has a AAA Four Diamond rating, and has been called by at least one member of the food press "Louisville's best restaurant." That, of course, is subject to opinion, but there is little argument about the quality of its beef, especially the rib eye steak, grilled to perfection, and the scope of its wine list — more than 200 selections. Likewise, its setting — which features lots of wooden pillars and stained glass — makes for an elegant dining experience, enhanced by a rule that more restaurants should follow — no cell phones!

335 West Broadway. (502) 583-1234. www.brownhotel.com/dining.
Dinner: Monday–Saturday, 6:00–9:00 p.m.
Reservations recommended.

EQUUS

It bills itself as a restaurant offering American regional cuisine and it delivers, especially with such dishes as 20-hour beef brisket with truffled mashed potatoes and onion rings, and shrimp Jenkins, a fried Carolina shrimp flavored with brown sugar, rosemary, Worcestershire, Tabasco, and bourbon. The wine list features some 300 selections.

122 Sears Ave. (502) 897-9721. www.equusrestaurant.com.
Dinner: Monday–Saturday, 6:00–10:00 p.m.

JACK FRY'S

This is the kind of restaurant that every city should have at least one of — noisy, collegial, a place where strangers at the bar waiting for a table become friends over a Wild Turkey bourbon. And that's just how Jack Fry would have liked it. A flamboyant lover of pugilists and the ponies, he opened the restaurant in 1933 and it quickly became an early version of today's sports bar. Those days are still in evidence with the black and white photos on the walls. Jack's dealings were sometimes unsavory — he was said to have conducted his bootlegging and bookmaking in a back room — but there's nothing unsavory about the dishes on the menu. Lobster crab cakes, Stilton salad, lamb chops with a rosemary natural jus, sinful chocolate soufflé cake, and peach shortcake are among the tempting offerings. As if the buzz from the patrons wasn't music enough, there's live jazz here from Tuesday–Saturday night.

1007 Bardstown Rd. (502) 452-9244. www.jackfrys.com.
Lunch: Monday–Friday, 11:00 a.m.–2:30 p.m.
Dinner: Monday–Thursday, 5:30–11:00 p.m.; Friday & Saturday,
5:30–midnight, and Sunday, 5:30–10:00 p.m.

JEFF RUBY'S STEAKHOUSE

This is a chophouse for the true steak lover. The dark rich interior — lots of leather and subdued lighting — complements the dry aged meats personally selected for the steakhouse, from the T-bones and New York strip to the Colorado lamb. But non-meat eaters need not despair. They offer a huge selection of fish dishes, salads, appetizers, and sides as well as an impressive sushi bar.

325 West Main St. (502) 584-0102. www.jeffruby.com/louisville
Dinner: Monday–Thursday, 5:00–10:00 p.m.;
Friday & Saturday, 5:00–11:00 p.m.

BISTRO LE RELAIS

Bowman Field airport may seem like a strange place for Louisville's most sophisticated French cuisine, but that's just what you get at Le Relais, located in the airport terminal. The menu features dishes such as moules marinieres (steamed mussels, shallots, and herbs in white wine), vichyssoise with small peas, vegetable cassoulet, cotelette d'agneau, and coquilles St. Jacques, with a wine list to match (the best of Bordeaux, Burgundy, and the Rhone region). And then there's the ambiance — very film noirish with its low lighting and Art Deco touches such as burled wood and banquette seating. It's the kind of place where the patrons all look as if they should be sucking the olives out of their martinis, and the waiters all should look like Humphrey Bogart (or Peter Lorre or Sydney Greenstreet or any of the other male characters in the movie *Casablanca*). If you can stand any more ambiance, try dining on the outdoor deck and watching the planes take off and land (Humphrey Bogart suddenly morphs into Charles Lindburgh, who actually landed The Spirit of St. Louis here once).

2817 Taylorsville Rd. at Bowman Field.

(502) 451-9020. www.lerelaisrestaurant.com.

Dinner: Tuesday–Sunday,

beginning at 5:30 p.m.

LILLY'S

Lilly's calls itself "an American bistro," and indeed it would be hard to find a chef as devoted to local products as Kathy Cary. Cary's menu is driven by what is available locally, and she supplements produce from local purveyors with that grown in her own organic garden. *Gourmet* magazine describes eating here as "like being in the dining room of a gentleman farmer," and Cary's style of cooking has earned her five invitations to cook at New York City's prestigious James Beard House. Dishes such as roasted heirloom pumpkin soup topped with a fig quenelle and seared scallops in mango-tarragon beurre blanc show why.

1147 Bardstown Rd. (502) 451-0447. www.lillyslapeche.com.
Lunch: Tuesday–Saturday, 11:00 a.m.–3:00 p.m.
Dinner: Tuesday–Saturday, 5:30–10:00 p.m.
Reservations recommended.

LYNN'S PARADISE CAFÉ

If, in a fantasy world, the late Salvadore Dali and Dolly Parton had teamed up to open a restaurant, they might have come up with something like this. Unfortunately for them, Lynn Winter beat them to it. The unusual (an understatement) décor begins outside with an eight-foot red coffeepot and the Gallopalooza horse and continues inside — patrons can have their picture taken inside a giant fork and spoon. Speaking of patrons, don't be surprised to see an entire table of them sporting fake clown noses or even dining in their pajamas. Lynn encourages her guests to let their inner child out for a few hours. She also advocates creative food, which might mean gargantuan western and Popeye omelets for breakfast, Mom's meatloaf with all the trimmings or catfish fried in a Cajun-spiced Weisenberger cornmeal breading for lunch, and the Paradise hot brown or pecan chicken in Woodford Reserve mustard maple cream sauce for dinner. If you're only in Louisville for a short time, by all means, make this one of your stops.

984 Barrett Ave. (502) 583-3447. www.lynnsparadisecafe.com.
Monday–Friday, 7:00 a.m.–10:00 p.m.;
Saturday & Sunday, 8:00 a.m.–10:00 p.m.

NAPA RIVER GRILL

As its name indicates, the menu is inspired by California's Napa River region, which means lots of fresh local ingredients and a blend of ethnic influences. I haven't eaten here yet, but a friend swears by the Caesar salad served in a toast bowl made of Parmesan cheese, the short rib appetizer on a bed of mushroom risotto, and the creamy tomato soup served with a puff pastry on top.

1211 Herr La. (502) 423-5822. www.napariverlouisville.com.
Lunch: Monday–Friday, 5:00–10:00 p.m.
Dinner: Monday–Thursday, 5:00–10:00 p.m.; Friday & Saturday,
5:00–11:00 p.m., and Sunday, 5:00–9:00 p.m.

NORTH END CAFÉ

A funky favorite in two renovated shotgun houses where the food is complemented by the work of up-and-coming local artists and a local DJ performing Thursdays–Saturdays. The café serves breakfast, lunch, and dinner so you can make your way through cornmeal buttermilk pancakes to curry sauté to flat iron steak or seared lemon sole roulade.

1722 Frankfort Ave. (502) 896-8770. www.northendcafe.com.
Sunday, Tuesday, Wednesday, and Thursday, 8:00 a.m.–10:00 p.m.
and Friday and Saturday, 8:00 a.m.–11:00 p.m.

THE OAK ROOM

Kentucky's only AAA Five Diamond restaurant, the Oak Room in the Seelbach Hotel is elegant and formal in atmosphere (even Al Capone used to dress up in his best duds to eat here), but casual and innovative in its cuisine. Classic dishes get a modern interpretation, and the chef uses locally grown or raised produce and infuses it with touches from around the globe.

500 Fourth St. (502) 585-3200. www.seelbachhilton.com.
Dinner: Tuesday–Saturday, 5:30–10:00 p.m.; Sunday brunch,
10:00 a.m.–2:00 p.m. Reservations recommended.

PROOF ON MAIN

This arty restaurant in 21C Museum Hotel has, since its opening a few years back, received rave reviews from New York to Hong Kong. Part of it has to do with the cachet of the hotel itself; most, however, is due to the kitchen artistry of Chef Michael Paley. His modern America-meets-Tuscany menu features dishes such as pan-roasted scallops with caramelized spaghetti squash, minted pea bruschetta with artisan bread, pine nuts, and arugula, and daily specials that aren't in the least "blue plate" — ranging from handmade gnocchi to rabbit cacciatore. The restaurant's décor matches the vibrancy of the food — hand-blown glass pendant lights sparkling from the ceiling and glass votives, bronze statuary in the lively bar area, and a unique outdoor chandelier gracing the front entrance.

702 West Main St. (502) 217-6360. www.proofonmain.com.
Lunch: Monday–Friday, 11:00 a.m.–2:00 p.m. Dinner: Monday–
Thursday, 5:30–10:00 p.m.; Friday & Saturday, 5:30–11:00 p.m.
Breakfast and late night bar menu also available.

SEVICHE

Chef Anthony Lamas may have been influenced in the kitchen by his Mexican mother and his Puerto Rican father, but don't expect to find tacos cluttering up his menu — unless, of course, you order the mahi mahi taco with green cabbage, lime aioli, and pico de gallo. Likewise, he doesn't do tamales but does do Feijoada, a Brazilian dish that combines black beans, smoked meat, sausage, rice, manioc, and braised greens. Make no mistake — this is stylish, sophisticated Latin food.

1538 Bardstown Rd. (502) 473-8560. www.sevicherestaurant.com.
Dinner: Sunday & Monday, 5:00–9:00 p.m.;
Tuesday–Thursday, 5:00–10:00 p.m., and
Friday & Saturday, 5:00–11:00 p.m.

610 MAGNOLIA

Located in historic Old Louisville, the restaurant combines Southern hospitality with urban chic. The décor features wooden beams, mullioned windows, and French doors leading to a garden patio, while Frette linens, Riedel crystal, and polished mahogany tables complete the ambiance. Chef Edward Lee's cooking has been lauded in *Southern Living* and *GQ* magazines and on CBS television, and you can experience it for yourself in his three-, four-, and six-course dinners.

610 Magnolia. (502) 636-0783.
www.610magnolia.com. Dinner: Thursday, Friday, and Saturday nights only, 6p.m.–closing. Reservations required.

VINCENZO'S

At this long-time Louisville institution, you get classic Italian dishes prepared with passion and amore. Try the several different kinds of risotto, the veal parmigiano, or the lasagna bolognese. The setting is as elegant as the food.

150 South Fifth St. (502) 580-1350.
www.vincenzositalianrestaurant.com.
Lunch: Monday–Friday, 11:30 a.m.–2:00 p.m.
Dinner: Monday–Saturday, 5:00–10:00 p.m.

WILD EGGS

Eating here will convince you your mother was right when she said, "Breakfast is the most important meal of the day." There's the usual fare: house-baked buttermilk biscuits and sausage gravy and old-fashioned oatmeal, but there are also more adventurous alternatives — wild berry crepes with sweetened cream cheese, blueberry sorghum, and cinnamon, or crispy waffles with caramel coffee sauce, chocolate-dipped espresso beans, and whipped cream. And oh yes, they serve lunch too.

Two locations: 3985 Dutchmans La. in St. Matthews
(502) 893-8005 and 1311 Herr La. in Westport Village.
(502) 618-2866. www.crackinwildeggs.com.

Z'S FUSION

Fusion has become an overused culinary term in recent years, with some chefs thinking that if they mix oil and vinegar then it's fusion. At Z's, dishes such as lemongrass mussels, rock shrimp potstickers, tandori-spiced swordfish, and miso-roasted pulled pork with ginger-scallion honey sauce will convince you that they really do know the meaning of the term fusion.

115 South Fourth St. (502) 855-8000. www.zsfusion.com.
Lunch: Monday–Friday, 11:00 a.m.–2:30 p.m.

Dinner: Monday–Thursday, 5:00–10:00 p.m.; Friday & Saturday, 5:00–11:00 p.m.; Sunday, 5:00–9:00 p.m.

Z'S OYSTER BAR & STEAKHOUSE

The sister restaurant to Z's Fusion, you can expect to get what the name says — plump oysters from the Gulf Coast and the Pacific Coast and every type of beef you can imagine, hand-cut to order. The wine list is huge — some 600 different wines. Recipient of a Wine Spectator Award of Excellence and a AAA 4 Diamond rating.

101 Whittington Pkwy. (502) 429-8000. www.zsoyster.com. Same hours of operation as Z's Fusion.

Midway/Versailles

BISTRO LA BELLE

The restaurant, which opened in 1998, was instrumental in helping put Midway on the culinary map. It features locally grown or raised products such as pan fried organic liver from Pike Valley Farms, tossed with red onions, bacon, baby spinach, sweet mustard dressing, and topped with Capriole goat cheese, and cheese grits made with flour from nearby Weisenberger Mill.

121 Main St., Midway. (859) 846-4233. http://bistrolabelle. googlepages.com. Dinner: Wednesday–Saturday, 5:30–9:00 p.m.

CLEVELAND'S

Executive Chef Jared Richardson has made this restaurant in the

Woodford Inn a bastion of Kentucky cooking. That means fried catfish and pork chops marinated in bourbon barbecue sauce and served with side dishes such as stone-ground grits, slow cooked greens, corn pudding, and fried apples. You can dine in the main dining room or to make it even more of a Southern tradition, on the sun porch. The adjoining Bourbon Bar features more than 50 premium bourbons.

140 Park St., Versailles. (859) 879-6062. www.woodfordinn.com. Lunch: Monday–Saturday, 11:00 a.m.–2:00 p.m. Dinner: Monday–Saturday, 5:00–9:00 p.m.; Sunday brunch, 11:00 a.m.–2:00 p.m.

HEIRLOOM

Another of the culinary hot spots on Main Street. One dish that has received raves from Wendy Miller, food writer for the *Herald-Leader*, is the sautéed chicken livers, paired with rich and slightly tart lemon-ricotta ravioli, with a suggestion of garlic, basil, and crème fraiche.

125 Main St., Midway. (859) 846-5565. www.heirloommidway.com. Lunch: Tuesday–Saturday, 11:30 a.m.–2:00 p.m. Dinner: Tuesday–Saturday, 5:30 p.m.–closing. Wine tastings and a bar menu are available Tuesday–Saturday, 3:00–5:00 p.m. Reservations recommended.

HOLLY HILL INN

Ouita Michel is one of the commonwealth's most famous chefs and this 1845 National Register property, which she owns with her husband and fellow CIA-trained chef Chris, has become a pilgrimage spot for foodies. Holly Hill is the very definition of what a country inn should be — tree-shaded, large front porch, linen tablecloths, candles, and fresh flowers, but — lovely as it is — that's all window dressing. The core of the inn is Ouita's inventive menu. Try the golden brown butternut squash bisque, the trout meuniere, bathed in buttermilk and rolled in pecan-crumbed corn meal, the gratin of local poussin and creamy macaroni (forget the Velveeta; this macaroni is gratineed in gruyere) and the trio of Kentucky farmhouse cheeses. Holly Hill's "spring in the bluegrass" lunch menu is extremely popular with the local clientele.

426 North Winter St. Midway. (859) 846-4732.
www.hollyhillinn.com.
Lunch: Wednesday–Saturday, 11:30 a.m.–2:00 p.m.
Dinner: Wednesday–Saturday, 5:30–closing; Sunday brunch,
11:30 a.m.–2:30 p.m. Reservations recommended.

WALLACE STATION

If restaurants, like cats, have nine lives, then Wallace Station has gone through four of them. Beginning as a train depot, then a post office and country store, it is now an upscale bakery and sandwich shop. Located near Midway in the midst of horse country, Wallace Station is owned by CIA-trained chef Jared Richardson and his wife Paige, who — in addition to their sandwiches, salads, and pastries (the best blueberry muffins ever) — do lots of fun stuff (fried chicken night every Monday and the occasional Friday night fish fry).

3854 Old Frankfort Pike. (859) 846-5161.
Hours vary, so it's best to check before going.

THREE SUNS BISTRO

Don't be put off by the fact that it is located in a small strip mall; the food is anything but ordinary. Eclectic is the word for the menu that changes constantly. Some of the dishes aren't exactly conventional — try pecan fried chicken with a drizzle of sweet praline sauce. Order it anyway. FYI: Their appetizers are hearty enough to serve as a complete meal.

298 East Brannon Rd. in Brannon's Crossing Shopping Center. (859) 245-0048. www.threesunsbistro.com. Lunch: Monday–Thursday, 11:00 a.m.–3:00 p.m., Dinner: Monday–Thursday, 5:00–9:00 p.m.; Friday, 5:00–10:00 p.m.; Saturday, noon–10:00 p.m.

OLD STONE INN

If you're looking for a place to combine good food with history, this is it. Begun in the late 1700s and thought to have been completed around 1817, the building has served as a stagecoach stop, tavern, and private home, and since the 1920s, a restaurant. Among the famous that have congregated at this National Historic Landmark are President Andrew Jackson and Revolutionary War hero the Marquis de Lafayette. While the white tablecloths and uniformed wait staff may lead you to expect haute cuisine, the inn is devoted to regional cooking at its best — think bourbon barrel pork chops with apple cider glaze and baked Weisenberger white cheddar grits or fried chicken with mashed potatoes and milk gravy and what some diners have called "the best southern-style green beans you have ever tasted." And I don't know who Grandma Mary is, but her chicken livers are sure worth trying. This is not the place to bring the calorie counter.

⋄⋄⋄⋄⋄⋄ ⋄⋄⋄⋄⋄⋄

6905 Shelbyville Rd., Simpsonville. (502) 722-8200.
www.old-stone-inn.com.
Lunch: Thursday and Friday, 11:00 a.m.– 2:00 p.m.
Dinner: Monday–Saturday, 4:00 p.m.–10:00 p.m.

After Dark

There's no reason why you should head back to your hotel to watch *The Tonight Show* after you've finished dining at one of the region's fine restaurants. Both Lexington and Louisville have a plethora of nightlife options, of which I've listed a few of the most popular.

LEXINGTON

In the past, Lexington — unless you were a college student hitting the weekend fraternity parties — was something of an after-dark wasteland. No longer. In recent years bars and live music clubs have been sprouting like mushrooms, and the renaissance doesn't appear to be ending any time soon.

If Woo-Man and the Banana, Thriving Ivory, and Jason and the Punknecks sound like the titles of B movies, then you're probably not the target audience for **The Dame (367 West Main St., 859-231-7263, www.dameky.com)**, Lexington's Live (and liveliest) Music Hall. The bands that perform here seven nights a week run the gamut from rhythm & blues and hip hop to punk rock and rockabilly. As noted, the crowd here tends to be on the younger side, although some acts do draw an older crowd.

Pulse (257 West Short St., 859-552-4398). Lexington's most diverse entertainment venue has live bands, open-mic night (Tuesdays), cabaret shows featuring entertainers in drag, a pool table and lounge, and nightly happy hour (or therapy, as they call it here) from 4:00–9:00 p.m.

At **Redmon's (269 West Main St., 859-252-5802, www.larryredmon.com)**, troubadour Larry Redmon and his acoustic guitar take fans on a soulful musical journey through the Southland, from Appalachia to the Mississippi Delta. Thursday–Saturday. $5 cover. Reservations recommended.

Bluegrass Tavern (115 Cheapside, 859-389-6664, www.thebluegrasstavern.com) is Central Kentucky's premier bourbon bar, with some 178 different kinds. Open until 2:30 a.m. Monday–Saturday.

Bakers 360 (201 East Main St., 859-523-7797, www.bakers360.us) is a combination restaurant (specializing in steaks and seafood) and nightclub. Located on the 15th floor of the Chase Bank Building, it offers unparalleled views of downtown Lexington, and is definitely the place to see and be seen (it even has a swank VIP section). Open until 2:30 a.m. Thursday–Saturday, and until midnight Monday–Wednesday.

Victorian Square is fast becoming the city's entertainment hub, with three spots vying for the late-night crowd. **Lower 48 (401 West Main St., enter through Atrium of Victorian Square, www.lower48bar.com)** is an underground club that stays open until 2:30 a.m., offering hot music and cold spirits. **De Vassa (401 West Main St., 859-455-9139)** is Lexington's premier tapas bar, with live music Wednesday through Saturday. At the **Penguin Dueling Piano Bar (517 West Main St., 859-327-3333, www.penguinpianobar.com)** two baby grand pianos face each other on the stage, and the entertainers, brought in from around the country, have a repertoire of thousands of songs from the past five decades. By the end of the evening, the audience is usually singing along with them.

Just next to deSha's restaurant in Victorian Square is a gem of a pub that the prestigious *Whiskey Magazine* calls one of the three best whiskey bars in the world — yep, the world. Bourbon rules at the **Horse & Barrel (101 North Broadway, 859-259-3771)** — from cheap (Ancient Age at $4.25) to steep (Pappy Van Winkle's 23-year-old Reserve at $32). You can also get good pub grub — Shepherd's Pie and Fish and Chips accompanied by Guinness on tap.

Natasha's Café (112 Esplanade, 859-259-2754, www.beetnik.com) serves an eclectic menu of dishes that span cooking cultures from the Middle East to middle Europe, but it's as an entertainment venue that it really shines. The entertainment choices are as eclectic as the menu — one night it might be the Radoku Gypsy Dancers; on another, it's the Bats, an all-female band; and on still another, it could be a theatrical presentation of "The Mystery of Irma Veep." Truly one of Lexington's most innovative spots, it will put you in mind of New York's Soho or Tribeca districts.

Two of Lexington's newest hot spots are **The Tin Roof (303 South Limestone, 859-317-9111) and Blu Lounge and Soundbar (208 South Limestone, 859-523-6338, www.soundbarlex. com)**. The former, located in a converted Huddle House diner on the UK campus, has live music and food. The latter, in an Art Deco building with a lovely patio, is a combination lounge and dance bar. Soundbar has plasma video screens with the latest music videos, and on weekends, guest DJs. Blu Lounge claims to be "bringing back the art of the cocktail."

For two completely different experiences, try **Comedy Off Broadway (161 Lexington Green Cir., 859-271-5653, www. comedyoffbroadway.com)**, named one of the top comedy clubs in North America by the Professional Comedians Association, and **Red Barn Radio (161 North Mill St., www.redbarnradio.com)**, where you can experience the music of Kentucky, from bluegrass to the folk music of Appalachia, in live tapings every Wednesday night at 7:00 p.m. in the Performance Hall at Arts Place. Cost is $5 and reservations are necessary.

LOUISVILLE

4th Street Live Entertainment District, a pedestrian mall in downtown, is Ground Zero for nightlife, with no fewer than a dozen bars and clubs for you to choose from — from sports bars to nightclubs that would be at home in the Big Apple or South Beach. A few of them include:

Howl at the Moon (502-562-9400, www.howlatthemoon. com) claims to be home to the World's Greatest Rock 'N' Roll Dueling Piano Show.

The Sports & Social Club (502-568-1400, www.thesports-andsocialclub.com) is a relaxed sports bar in a tavern setting, offering pub food, great drinks, and, of course, sports viewing on wide-screen TVs.

Angel's Rock Bar (502-540-1461, www.angelsrockbar-ky. com). There's nothing angelic about this spot, which bills itself as "part lounge, part club, and all rock and roll." Among its features are a 130-foot bar and a live music stage.

If you are looking to go around the world, you can do it right here at 4th Street Live. At **Tengo Sed Cantina (502-540-1461, www.tengosed-ky.com)** it's "all fiesta and no siesta," while at **Ri Ra Irish Pub (502-587-1825, www.rira.com)** you can enjoy everything from pub quizzes to traditional Celtic music in an authentic 1900s Victorian pub that was disassembled and shipped from County Wicklow, Ireland, to Louisville.

You know that a place offering drinks called Sex on the Beach, Shock Treatment, Monster Melon, and Attitude Improvement isn't going to be a quiet piano bar. Welcome to **Wet Willie's (502-581-1332, www.wetwillies.com)** where it's spring break all year round.

Music, art, fashion, and five-star service combine at **Hotel (502-540-1461, www.hotel-kentucky.com),** one of the most sophisticated clubs in the 4th Street Live area. Put on your best duds and make like you're walking the red carpet.

No matter where you start out, you'll probably end up at **Maker's Mark Bourbon Lounge (502-568-9009, www.makerslounge.com).** The unofficial starting point for the "Urban Bourbon Trail," it boasts design features such as custom art glass and a 57-foot bar outlined in marble, as well as 60 custom-distilled bourbons.

If you still have the strength after exhausting all of 4th Street Live's entertainment offerings, here are two more Louisville institutions:

Stevie Ray's Blues Bar (230 East Main St., 502-582-9945, www.stevieraysbluesbar.com) is the only venue in Louisville to bring in nationally known blues singers and musicians.

The Phoenix Hill Tavern (644 Baxter Ave., 502-589-4957, www.phoenixhill.com) is the recipient of 18 "Best of Louisville" awards for nightlife. It has two floors with five bars, from a first floor saloon to the rooftop garden, complete with greenery, chandelier, and softly lit fountain. If you can't find what you're looking for here, then you aren't trying.

13

Where to Shop

No guidebook can hope to introduce readers to all the places in an area that make for good shopping. It is my intent in this chapter to introduce you to those spots that offer merchandise of extremely high quality or those that specialize in products unique to Kentucky.

Lexington

BOB MICKLER'S LIFESTYLE & PERFORMANCE RIDING APPAREL

Since 1949, this has been the place to go for English-inspired casual clothing and footwear, with a specialty in riding apparel for both adults and children. You can get your breeches, chaps, helmets, coats, and accessories here as well as a variety of equipment for your horse. Even if you're not a rider, you can choose from a line of specialty gifts for the equestrian in your life.

1093 West High St. (859) 254-3814. www.bobmicklers.com.

CROSS GATE GALLERY

The two-story pink Greek Revival-style building just east of downtown is the place to go in Lexington for equine-related sporting art. Throughout its 11,000 square feet and two floors of gallery space, Cross Gate exhibits the work of top artists from both the United States and Europe. The gallery's high-profile customers include the Fasig-Tipton Company, Keeneland Race Course, and the Breeders' Cup. In addition to high-quality paintings and prints, Cross Gate also offers custom framing.

509 East Main St. (859) 233-3856. www.crossgategallery.com.
Monday–Friday from 9:00 a.m.–5:30 p.m. and
Saturday from 9:00 a.m.–1:00 p.m.

GALLERY B

This Lexington establishment is known for quality fine art by locally and nationally recognized artists and for custom framing. Although it offers an eclectic range of art, it has a large selection of equine and equine-related pieces.

145 West Main St. (859) 233-0843. www.galleryblexington.com.
Tuesday–Friday from 10:30 a.m.–5:30 p.m. and
Saturday from 10:30 a.m.–6:00 p.m.

GREENTREE CLOSE

Visitors stumbling on to this leafy enclave on West Short Street in the historic downtown area could be forgiven for thinking that they might be in London, Paris, or New York City, so elegant are the quartet of establishments that comprise Greentree Close.

L.V. Harkness and Company was begun by Meg Jewett-Leavitt and named in honor of her great-grandfather, Lamon Vanderburg Harkness, a 19th-century shareholder in the Standard Oil Company and noted owner of Walnut Hall Farm.

Jewett shares her ancestor's love for beautiful objets d'art, and one look around the elegantly appointed showrooms of L.V. Harkness will be enough to convince you that this is no ordinary gift shop. From formal tableware and linens to home furnishings and accessories to equine-related merchandise, the names are synonymous with quality — Meissen, Baccaret, Faberge, Lalique, and Hermes. The store's lovely rooftop gardens were designed by noted Kentucky garden designer Jon Carloftis, who has also designed gardens for such famous folk as film stars Julianne Moore and Edward Norton and television and movie producer Jerry Bruckheimer and his wife Linda.

At the opposite end of the Close from L.V. Harkness is Belle Maison Antiques. Owner Debbie Chamblin, a Francophile, travels to France several times a year in search of the most distinctive pieces. Her travels yield an interesting selection of fine furniture (beds, chairs, armoires) and furnishings (chandeliers and mirrors) as well as linens and dishes. If you're lucky on the day of your visit, you might be greeted by Chamblin's "assistant" — an adorable King Charles spaniel who answers to Riley.

Tucked in between L.V. Harkness and Belle Maison is the newest store, Trillium. In contrast to the other two, this sleek emporium offers furniture and accessories for a more contemporary lifestyle.

Finally, across the parking lot is Greentree Antiques and Tearoom. Here, you can shop for what is perhaps the most traditional of the merchandise offered at the three properties specializing in antiques, as well as enjoy a proper tea in the elegant tearoom. A typical tea menu features such fare as Greentree classic cucumber, dill and shrimp tea sandwiches, tomato and basil scone with Parmesan butter, and chocolate pots de crème, Greentree French-filled wafers, and strawberry cream cake, with, of course, the appropriate assortment of teas to accompany the food.

L.V. Harkness is located at 531 West Short St. (859) 225-7474.
www.lvharkness.com. Monday–Friday, 10:00 a.m.–6:00 p.m.;
Saturday, 10:00 a.m.–5:00 p.m.

Belle Maison is at 525 West Short St. (859) 252-9030.
www.bellemaisonantiques.com. Tuesday–Saturday,
10:00 a.m.–4:00 p.m.

Trillium is at 525 West Short St. (859) 255-1010.
www.trilliumstyle.com. Tuesday–Saturday,
10:00 a.m.–5:00 p.m.

Greentree Antiques & Tearoom is at 521 West Short St.
(859) 455-9660. www.greentreetearoom.com. Tuesday–Saturday,
10:00 a.m.–4:00 p.m.
Reservations for tea are required.

JOSEPH-BETH BOOKSELLERS

One of the nation's strongest and most prosperous independent booksellers, with stores in Cincinnati, Pittsburgh, Nashville, Memphis, and Charlotte, Joseph-Beth's flagship store is located here in Lexington. The 40,000-square-foot bookstore is a bibliophile's paradise. It has two floors of books — including a section

DID YOU KNOW

The nation's winningest college basketball
program, the University of Kentucky Wildcats,
have seven National Championship banners
hanging at Rupp Arena in Lexington.

just for children's literature, a music department, a boutique gift section, and the Bronte Café, with both indoor and outdoor seating. The store's frequent book signings have attracted such high-profile authors as Anne Rice, Stephen King, Paula Deen, Jimmy Carter, and Hillary Clinton.

Lexington Green, off Nicholasville Rd. (859) 273-2911. www.josephbeth.com.

KEENELAND GIFT SHOP

The gift shop at Keeneland Race Course has been described as "a little slice of equine heaven," with gifts suitable "from head to hoof" and "from weanlings to adults." This is definitely the place to go for anything with a horsey motif — from apparel to artwork, from the home to the golf course. Some merchandise is whimsical — the jockey bobbleheads, for example — while some is exquisite — beautiful paintings by famed New Zealand artist Peter Williams, who has become Keeneland's de facto artist-in-residence.

Located on the grounds of Keeneland Race Course, 4201 Versailles Rd. (859) 288-4236. www.keeneland.stores.truition.com. Hours vary; the shop is open longer during racing season and the horse sales.

KENTUCKY HORSE PARK GIFT SHOP & TACK SHOP

Another high-end shop for equine-related merchandise. Located in the visitor's center at the Horse Park, it specializes in items for all horse lovers, including apparel for children and adults, equine books, art and statuary, Horse Park and Kentucky souvenirs, and 2010 World Equestrian Games official merchandise. The Tack Shop offers both equine necessities (stable and grooming products and feed supplements) and Kentucky Horse Park custom products (saddles and leather goods, riding hardware).

⬦⬦⬦⬦⬦⬦·⬦⬦⬦⬦·⬦⬦·⬦⬦·⬦⬦

4089 Iron Works Pkwy. (859) 259-4234. www.kyhorsepark.com. 9:00 a.m.–5:00 p.m. daily.

Berea

Designated the "arts and crafts capital of Kentucky" (see Chapter 8), this small community about a half-hour from Lexington is a shopper's paradise, particularly for those in search of folk art. In addition to the shops that face College Square and the shops and galleries that line Old Town Artisans' Village, it is also home to the Kentucky Artisan Center.

For traditional folk arts and crafts, go to Appalachian Fireside Gallery, Log House Craft Gallery, and the Kentucky Artisan Center. On College Square, the Bluetail Fly specializes in unique toys and gifts, and The Gallery is Berea's first co-op art space, featuring the works of several regional artists.

Old Town Artisans' Village offers an eclectic shopping experience — traditional glass vases and ornaments (The Glass Studio), sculptures of amazingly life-like dolls (Images of Santa), pewter jewelry and home accessories (Gastineau Studio), custom-made hardwood furniture (Haley-Daniels), and the beadwork of nationally known designer Jimmy Lou Jackson (Hot Flash Beads).

If you are looking for pottery, Honeysuckle Vine has Bybee Pottery, and just east of town, at Tater Knob Pottery, you can watch potters create beautiful pieces on a wheel. (You can get directions to Tater's Knob at the Berea Welcome Center in Old Town.)

Frankfort

Paul Sawyier is to Kentucky what Georgia O'Keefe is to New Mexico. Arguably the commonwealth's most famous painter, he became enamored of the Impressionist movement after it was formally introduced in the United States at the 1893 Chicago World's Fair, and he subsequently became known as one of the first American Impressionists.

Although born in Ohio in 1865, Sawyier moved to Frankfort as a child, and it was the bucolic Central Kentucky countryside that inspired most of the 3,000 original oils and watercolors he was known to have painted during his career (only half of which have ever been located or accounted for).

If Monet had Giverny and Turner and Constable had the marshlands of England's East Anglia, Sawyier had Frankfort, Elkhorn Creek, and the Kentucky River; he lived on the latter for five years on a houseboat, painting scenes up and down the river, mainly between Shaker Village and Camp Nelson.

His passion for Kentucky's waterways is apparent in such contrasting works as *A View on Dix River*, which is infused with warm yellow tones, and *Elkhorn Reflections*, a study in cool blues and greens. One of his river-themed works, *Boys Wading*, painted while he was living on the houseboat, is noteworthy in that one of the boys is rumored to be Howard Hughes, who vacationed as a child on that stretch of Elkhorn Creek.

If Sawyier was infatuated with river life, he was equally enamored of Kentucky's capital city. His cityscapes of Frankfort, especially *Rainy Day in Frankfort*, evoke the 19th-century street scenes of Paris, a mecca for European Impressionists. In this canvas, the damp chill of a winter afternoon is almost palpable. By contrast, he was equally adept at capturing the warm autumnal hues of a late fall day on Frankfort's Wapping Street.

The largest selection of Paul Sawyier works — some 300 framed canvases as well as a large inventory of unframed pieces — can be found at the Paul Sawyier Gallery, located at 3445 Versailles Road in Frankfort.

9:00 a.m.–5:00 p.m., Monday–Saturday.
(502) 695-5589.

Louisville

LOUISVILLE STONEWARE AND HADLEY POTTERY

Some yuppies and gen-xers think that modern pottery began with the founding of The Pottery Barn in Lower Manhattan some 60 years ago. Louisvillians know better. As far back as 1815, talented artisans were handcrafting pottery, using local clay meant to rival the finest English Spode and Wedgewood.

Today, that tradition continues at Louisville Stoneware. Its signature colors — blue, yellow, and white — are as well known to knowledgeable pottery collectors on this side of the pond as Wedgewood's blue and white is on the other side, and two of Louisville Stoneware's most popular designs — Pear and Bachelor Button (the latter with each of its blue flower petals painted by hand) are a fixture on Derby tables across the commonwealth.

Louisville Stoneware's history is as colorful as its design patterns. In the early 19th century, a few years after the Americans had battled the British in New Orleans during the War of 1812, company founder Jacob Lewis began his own battle with the British — this time at the kiln. Where his countrymen succeeded militarily, Lewis succeeded artistically, turning out jars, pitchers, mixing bowls, beer steins, and jugs. After Lewis left in the mid-19th century, following a squabble with Congress over land usage rights, the pottery went through a series of owners before being purchased in 1938 by John Taylor, son-in-law of the company's then owner.

It was during Taylor's tenure that the focus switched from crockery to one-of-a-kind dinnerware fit for the finest table, and its customer base expanded from regional to national. Louisville Stoneware could now be found on dinner tables from the White's house to the White House.

On a visit to Louisville Stoneware today, you can see the firing process (at temperatures in excess of 2,300 degrees) that enhances the pottery's beauty and durability. Then you can discover the history of pottery in the museum with its collection of rare ceramics dating back to the early 19th century. Finally, you can see how you stack up against the professionals by painting your own plate.

Hadley Pottery hasn't been around as long as Louisville Stoneware (having opened in 1940), but in the hearts of pottery enthusiasts it is equally admired. What began with Mary Alice Hadley applying her artistic talents to the making of a custom set of dishes for her houseboat on the Ohio River has turned into a business supplying patterned pieces to generations of Louisvillians. But Hadley's success didn't stop there. Today, thousands of dishes, cups, saucers, bowls, teapots, platters, and plates, as well as other accessories — all bearing the imprint M.A. Hadley — are sold in every U.S. state except Alaska and Idaho, as well as in Canada.

The Hadley ware is also made from native clay. The decoration is applied directly on the green or unfired clay, which is then fired only once, at a temperature of 2,150 degrees, following which the white overglaze is painted with its distinctive blues, greens, and rusts.

The pottery operation is housed in the original factory, and people come from all over the world to tour it and to scout for seconds and bargains in the sales room.

Louisville Stoneware has two locations, at 731 Brent St. (502-582-1900) and in the St. Matthews Mall, 5000 Shelbyville Rd. (502-895-9221). www.louisvillestoneware.com.

Hadley Pottery is located at 1570 Story Ave. (502-584-2171). www.hadleypottery.com.

Midway

A small community located about 15 minutes from Lexington, Midway has become known as a shopper's paradise, with colorful cottages housing shops, which specialize in merchandise ranging from imported Irish linens and sweaters to one-of-a-kind pieces of folk art. For more on the shops of Midway, see Chapter 8.

Mt. Sterling

RUTH HUNT CANDY COMPANY

If Rebecca-Ruth is the most famous name associated with Kentucky candy (see Chapter 8), Ruth Hunt isn't far behind. Likewise, if Rebecca Ruth is known for its bourbon balls, Ruth Hunt, who began the company in 1921, became famous for her Blue Monday. A creamy confection of dark chocolate and pulled cream in the center, it has doubtless gotten many a chocolate lover through his or her own "blue Mondays."

Here, at the main headquarters of Ruth Hunt Candies, the friendly staff, if they are not too busy, will be happy to show you the production process. Even if they are too busy — after all, they are the official candy makers for Churchill Downs and the Kentucky Derby — you'll still get the benefit of the heady aroma of thick chocolate, sweet cream, and roasting nuts that permeates the air.

550 North Maysville Rd. (859) 498-0676. www.ruthhuntcandy. com. Monday–Saturday 9:00 a.m.–5:30 p.m. and Sunday, 1:00–5:30 p.m. There is also a Lexington location at 2313 Woodhill Dr. in the Woodhill Shopping Center. (859) 268-1559.

Richmond

BYBEE POTTERY

At first glance, the cabin some eight miles east of Richmond in southern Madison County would appear to have seen better days, and the product it has turned out for nearly 200 years isn't the most elegant of its kind, often irregularly formed and unevenly glazed. But for collectors everywhere, the name Bybee represents the Holy Grail of pottery making.

The oldest existing pottery west of the Allegheny Mountains, Bybee has been operated by five generations of the Cornelison family, who use the same rich yellow clay from the banks of the Kentucky River for making their dinnerware and decorative pottery that was used by the early settlers at Fort Boonesborough in making crude dishes.

Bybee is the last of the original potteries that once flourished in this area. The others, so history tells us, were destroyed during the Civil War by Confederate General John Hunt Morgan's guerilla raiders in retaliation for their pro-Union sympathies. Bybee was spared, so the story goes, because one of the potters, an immigrant, was known to have Confederate leanings.

Visitors can tour the building and talk to the artisans as they fire the clay and mold it into various shapes.

The Cornelison family has opened Little Bit of Bybee Pottery in Middleton, a Louisville suburb, as the showroom and sales operation for the pottery. Tours are also available here.

Bybee Pottery is located in Madison County, eight miles east of the Richmond Bypass on Ky 52 at Mile Marker 21. (859) 369-5350. Monday–Friday, 8:00 a.m.–noon and 12:30–3:00 p.m.

Little Bit of Bybee Pottery is located at 11617 Main St., Middleton. (502) 245-0557. www.bybeepottery.com. Monday–Saturday 9:30 a.m.–5:00 p.m. and in November and December, Sundays noon–5:00 p.m.

Shelbyville

WAKEFIELD-SCEARCE GALLERIES

Where Misses Juliet and Harriett Poynter once operated a finishing school for young ladies can now be found a gallery specializing in the finest of British antiques.

There has been a school on this site since 1825 when Julia Tevis founded Science Hill Academy, which, as its name implied, was for the purpose of teaching young ladies that they had more to learn than how to needlepoint a sampler up to 1939 when the school graduated its last class.

In later years, the Poynter sisters (no relation to the singing duo) took over instruction at the school, and while it maintained its reputation as one of the nation's best preparatory schools, the Misses Poynter were nonetheless, sticklers for etiquette. As one story goes, a young lady — after attending a party in town — thanked her hostess by telling her that she had enjoyed herself immensely, whereupon Miss Juliet chastised her by saying, "You do not go to a party to enjoy yourself; you go to enjoy others."

Today, Science Hill is a complex of six boutiques surrounding an interior courtyard and a restaurant, the Georgian Room, which specializes in American food with a Kentucky slant served in 19th-century surroundings. While the shops sell everything from men's and women's fashions to linens and silk floral arrangements, antiques are the drawing card — specifically the antiques at the Wakefield-Scearce Galleries. This gallery — spread out over a number of elegant rooms — has one of the country's largest collections of antique English furniture and home décor as well as antique silver. This is definitely the place to go for that julep cup, but don't think you're going to get it cheaply.

525 Washington Ave. (502) 633-4382.
www.wakefield-scearce.com.
Monday–Saturday from 9:00 a.m.–5:00 p.m.

The Georgian Room is open for lunch daily, except Monday,
11:30 a.m.–2:30 p.m. and for dinner on Friday and Saturday
5:30–8:30 p.m. Dinner reservations are required and can
be made by calling (502) 633-2825.

Guided Trail Rides & Horse Rentals

Kentucky Horse Council, a non-profit organization dedicated to the protection, growth, and development of the equine industry in Kentucky, contributed to this list. For more information about Kentucky horse trails, visit www.KentuckyHorse.org.

Bannon Woods Farm trail rides through Jefferson County Forest. 11116 Dezern Ave., Fairdale. (502) 363-2372. www.BannonWoodsFarm.com

Barren River Lake Resort State Park guided trail rides. 1149 State Park Rd., Lucas. (270) 646-2151. parks.ky.gov/findparks/resortparks/br/

Big Red Stables, LLC, guided trail rides on Tennessee Walking horses. 1605 Jackson Pike, Harrodsburg. (859) 734-3118 or (502) 330-8798.

Carter Caves State Resort Park stables guided trail rides. 344 Caveland Dr., Olive Hill. (606) 286-4411. parks.ky.gov/findparks/resortparks/cf/

Cave Run Resort and Stables trails and horse rentals. 1051 McClain Cemetery Rd. #1, Salt Lick. (606) 638-3018. www.caverunresortandstables.com/stables.html

Jesse James Riding Stables guided trail rides. 3057 Mammoth Cave Rd., Cave City. (270) 773-2560. www.jessejamesridingstables.com

Kentucky Horse Park pony and horseback rides. 4089 Iron Works Pkwy., Lexington. (859) 233-4303. www.kyhorsepark.com

Little Big Horse Trails guided trail rides. 1100 East Hwy 524, LaGrange. (502) 222-1842. www.geocities.com/littlebighorsetrails/

McNeely Lake Park Riding Trails and Rental Horses. 6711 Mount Washington Rd., Louisville. Contact manager Diana Clute. (502) 224-1469. www.louisvilleky.gov/MetroParks/parks/mcneelylake/Mc-Neely_Horseback_riding.htm

Sugar Creek Resort trail and dinner rides. 5800 Sugar Creek Pike, Nicholasville. (859) 885-9359. www.sugarcreekresort.com/

Whispering Woods Riding Stable trail rides and horse rentals. 265 Wright La., Georgetown. (502) 570-9663. www.whisperingwoodstrails.com

Wranglers Riding Stables Land Between the Lakes guided trail rides. Golden Pond. (270) 924-2211.

Contact Information

Some handy contact information for the horse lover's ramble through the Bluegrass:

Kentucky Department of Tourism: (800) 225-8747. www.kentuckytourism.com

Lexington Convention & Visitors Bureau: (800) 845-3959. www.visitlex.com

Louisville Convention & Visitors Bureau: (888) LOUISVILLE. www.gotolouisville.com

Bardstown/Nelson County Tourist Commission: (800) 638-4877. www.visitbardstown.com

Berea Tourist Commission: (800) 598-5263. www.berea.com

Danville/Boyle County CVB: (800) 755-0076. www.danvillekentucky.com

Frankfort/Franklin Co. Tourism & Convention Center: (800) 960-7200. www.visitfrankfort.com

Harrodsburg/Mercer Co. Tourist Commission: (800) 355-9192. www.harrodsburg.com

Woodford County Tourism Commission: (859) 873-5122. www.woodfordchamber-ky.com

Index

About the Author

Patti Nickell is a freelance travel writer whose assignments have taken her to 101 countries and six continents, where she has gotten plenty of fodder for her bi-monthly travel features in the Lexington *Herald-Leader*.

Her articles have also appeared in numerous newspapers, including the *Washington Post*, *San Antonio Express News*, *Fort Worth Star Telegram*, *Dallas Morning News*, and *USA Today*, and in magazines such as *Keeneland* magazine, *Elite Traveler*, *Woman's Day*, *European Homes and Gardens*, *Atlanta Homes & Lifestyles*, *Las Vegas* magazine, *Forbes*, and *Forbes Asia*. In addition, she has contributed to Fodor's *Travel Guide* and television's The Travel Channel, and has done consulting work for the Kentucky Department of Tourism and the Lexington Convention & Visitors Bureau.

Prior to moving to Lexington, Patti lived in New Orleans, where she was a staff writer for *CityBusiness* newspaper, and contributed to *New Orleans* magazine, *Southern Woman*, *Gambit*, and the *Times-Picayune*, and served as travel editor of *New Orleans City Life* magazine. She was the recipient of the New Orleans Press Club's highest award for print journalism, the Alex Waller Award, for a piece that appeared in *New Orleans* magazine.

Horse Lover's Guide to Kentucky is her first book.

FEB 2 6 2010